Dolores Mosquera

Rough Diamonds

A glimpse into Borderline Personality Disorder

Informative manual for professionals, patients, and family members

Dolores Mosquera

Institute for the Treatment of Trauma and Personality Disorders (INTRA-TP)

Any kind of reproduction, distribution, public communication, and transformation of this content without authorization of the intellectual property owners is prohibited, unless otherwise provided by law. Infringement of these rights may constitute an offense against intellectual property.

Original title: *Diamantes en Bruto. Un acercamiento al Trastorno Límite de la Personalidad.*

Translation: Miriam Ramos Morrison

Illustrations: Nadia Santiago

Copyright © 2014, Dolores Mosquera Barral
Web: www.intra-tp.com
E-mail: doloresmosquera@gmail.com

ISBN-10: 1500868957

ISBN-13: 9781500868956

Table of Contents

Foreword

Part One. Glimpses into Borderline Personality Disorder

1. Introduction to Borderline Personality Disorder — 3
2. Common Features of People with Borderline Personality Disorder — 5
3. Borderline Personality Disorder: Understanding the DSM Criteria — 13
4. Borderline Personality Disorder from the Point of View of the Patients — 33

Part Two. Key Elements in Borderline Personality Disorder

5. Lack of Boundaries in People with Borderline Personality Disorder — 47
6. Negative Thoughts and Self-Destructive Behaviors — 51
7. Lack of Identity in People with Borderline Personality Disorder — 57
8. Dissociation and Borderline Personality Disorder — 63

Part Three. Assessment

9. Diagnosing Borderline Personality Disorder — 75
10. Defense Mechanisms — 81
11. Countertransference and Borderline Personality Disorder — 87

Part Four. Treatment

12. The Importance of Medication as a Complement to Therapy — 95
13. Group Therapy — 101
14. Family Therapy — 107
15. Psychotherapies for Borderline Personality Disorder — 109
16. Maintaining Improvement — 113

Appendix

A. Interview for Assessing the Presence of a possible Borderline Personality Disorder — 119
B. Therapeutic recommendations for the management of self-harming behaviors — 125
C. Principles that may be useful in individual and family approaches — 127

Acknowledgments — 135
References — 137

Dolores Mosquera *Rough Diamonds*

Foreword by Andrew M. Leeds

Knowledge is power. *Rough Diamonds I* offers essential information about Borderline Personality Disorder (BPD) in highly accessible language so that those affected by BPD can recognize the nature of the disorder and take steps to seek effective treatment. A companion workbook for patients and their therapists, already in use in Spain, *Rough Diamonds II* will be released in English in the near future.

The author of this practical and concise book, Dolores Mosquera, is an international authority on the treatment of personality disorders. Her INTRA-TP treatment centers in Spain are a national resource providing professional training in this speciality area for psychotherapists and psychiatric residents. She is a highly sought after speaker and trainer, offering workshops on the treatment of personality and dissociative disorders through Europe, as well as North and South America. Her integrative model is deeply informed by scholarly work in psychoanalysis, attachment theory, the theory of structural dissociation of the personality, and neuropsychology. She assimilates the richness of these models into simple and accessible language that reveals why she is such a popular and well-received presenter.

This is a down-to-earth book about a complex and often misunderstood condition. BPD is a serious mental illness estimated to occur in nearly 6% of the general population (Grant et al., 2008). While it is diagnosed more commonly in females, it most likely occurs as often in males who are often misdiagnosed or underdiagnosed with other conditions. The full range of BPD symptoms tends to be first noticed in adolescents and young adults, but its symptoms can start to appear in even young children. As the condition develops it has a major impact on quality of life of affected individuals, their families, friends and romantic partners.

Up to 70% of those with BPD report non-suicidal self-harm. Those with BPD are estimated to have a lifetime average of 4 psychiatric hospitalizations (Korzekwa et al., 2008). Those with BPD typically suffer from one or more co-occurring disorders including: anxiety disorders, such as posttraumatic stress disorder and panic attacks; bipolar disorder; major depressive disorder; eating disorders; other personality disorders and substance use disorders. It is these co-occurring disorders that are most likely to draw the attention of mental health professionals, who can, for a variety of reasons, fail to recognize or diagnose the presence of BPD.

The very name of this condition can seem mysterious and confusing, harkening back to misleading 19th century beliefs about a possible relationship between BPD and psychosis and to a psychoanalytic label for "untreatable neurotics" (Gunderson, 2009). *Rough Diamonds I* demystifies BPD, explaining the true nature of BPD symptoms and clarifying the actuality that effective treatment and good quality of life is possible for those who suffer from this condition. *Rough Diamonds I* has been a best selling book in Spain for many years where it has helped countless individuals and families learn the facts about this condition and to discover that effective treatment is available.

The origins of BPD can include both genetic and environmental factors, which lead to changes in brain function that are associated mood instability, insecure attachments and impulse control issues. Dolores Mosquera describes these and the other defining symptoms of BPD in clear and easily understood language that remains closely aligned to the latest DSM-5 criteria (APA, 2013). While BPD often emerges in those with histories of early childhood neglect and abuse, due to genetic factors, it can also occur in those offered secure attachments with a safe and stable home life.

Rough Diamonds I includes numerous personal narrative passages and drawings from those with BPD that provide tangible, identifiable elements for patients, families, friends, and therapists seeking to understand BPD. These personal elements illustrate the struggles of those with BPD and provide deep and compassionate glimpses into their inner lives and their healing journeys.

Rough Diamonds I provides invaluable information about the roles of medication and individual, group and family psychotherapies. Dolores Mosquera confronts and carefully examines the significant issue of therapist countertransference, which can lead to professional aversion to offer treatment and to treatment complications due to the strong reactions clinicians sometimes discover in themselves when treating those with BPD. Appendices include a structured interview for assessing the presence of BPD, recommendations for managing self-harming behaviors, and considerations in individual and family therapy settings.

Having observed at close hand the impact that Dolores Mosquera's professional and therapeutic work has had on so many, my hope is that you the reader will find within this marvelous volume the insights and guidance you seek.

Andrew M. Leeds

Dolores Mosquera *Rough Diamonds*

Part One
Glimpses into
Borderline Personality Disorder

Chapter 1
Introduction to Borderline Personality Disorder

Everyday, in emergency rooms, acute care wards, private practices, and mental health clinics, a large number of people (and their families) desperately seek help. They present with emotional chaos that interferes greatly with everyday life (difficulty focusing in school, keeping a job, constantly changing goals and aspirations, problems in personal relationships, and especially difficulty staying alive without getting hurt). Generally, they feel alone, misunderstood, confused, lost, incomplete, abandoned, and do not understand what is happening to them. These are particularly vulnerable and sensitive people.

Many of these people have an extensive clinical history, with frequent emergency room admissions due to self-harm, suicide attempts, substance abuse intoxication, or aggressive episodes, which endanger their lives and sometimes other people's lives as well. They claim to not be able to find their own identity or an explanation for their sense of emptiness and their angry and self-destructive impulsive reactions.

They are usually aware that their perception of reality differs significantly from that of other people. However, knowing this does not make them feel understood, but quite the opposite. They often express this with sentences such as: *"I know how I should be, what I should do, what would be normal to feel, but I'm incapable, I find it totally impossible."* This "weirdness awareness" and their inability to carry out what they know could work and improve their quality of life makes them feel great frustration and guilt.

It is common to find a wide range of diagnostic labels around them: anorexia, bulimia, depression, substance abuse, compulsive gambling, kleptomania, different anxiety disorders, bipolar disorder, etc. Any doubts that may arise regarding the correct diagnosis with these people during a hospital stay will increase if the patient's behavior is observed, due to their great capacity for mimicry and their desperate attempts to find an identity (their own identity). This leads them take the group of patients they have just joined as a reference (e.g., anorexia) and start copying and manifesting their symptomatology.

When they leave the hospital, they often carry this new and false identity with them. This creates a paradox of identity: Now she knows what she has. Now she feels like someone. She finally knows who she is ... (being anorexic is better than being nobody).

However, the problem does not end here, because they soon realize that this new identity does not fill their emptiness or explain their uncertainty. Their volatility, their lack of identity, their dependency, anger, impulsivity, and emptiness come back. Ultimately, without broader assessment and specific treatment, they will return to the

circle in which they will spin like a roulette wheel, jumping from diagnosis to diagnosis, when their true condition has a name: Borderline Personality Disorder (BPD).

This disorder has given rise to numerous theories in recent decades. Since its emergence as an official diagnosis in the DSM-III (*Diagnostic and Statistical Manual of Mental Disorders*) in 1980, there has been much research and it has generated much controversy among professionals, particularly regarding treatment and possible prognosis. No doubt this controversy has affected the often erroneous understanding of the disorder by those affected by it and their relatives. In addition, the range of emotional and behavioral responses in the patient, just like those they generate in therapists and other people around them, usually creates great confusion.

The mass media have not helped much in this regard either, as they have focused on the disorder's selling points, rather than disclosing its symptomatology in full. They bring up the "aggressive son," the "promiscuous woman," the "lying person who steals and insults," along with a number of testimonies that give rise to an image of "manipulative monsters" who assault, mistreat, and suffocate their family members.

In part, this has also led to a number of inaccurate diagnoses by professionals who are not well versed with the subject. Therefore, in many cases, we find people who are underserved and misunderstood and who jump from therapist to therapist, becoming confused and increasingly desperate.

This manual addresses these issues and provides suggestions that may be useful as tools for those professionals who deal with this disorder. It does not intend to redefine BPD, as there is much literature by professionals knowledgeable on the subject, and which is referenced throughout the manual and in the bibliographic appendix. But this manual does seek to establish realistic expectations about treatment and reduce the bad press regarding prognosis.

Chapter 2
Common Features of People with Borderline Personality Disorder

There are many factors to consider in the diagnosis and treatment of Borderline Personality Disorder (BPD), which will be addressed in sections 3 and 4 of this book. In this chapter, common characteristics that can be seen in many people with BPD will be described. Better understanding these characteristics may facilitate the diagnosis, case conceptualization, and treatment of this disorder.

INSTABILITY IN THEIR SENSE OF SELF

People with BPD usually have a variable self-image that is generally based on how they are perceived by others. When faced with criticism, they may feel bad, inept, or invalid. When they receive compliments, they can feel like a good person, someone great, etc.

This variability in their self-image or way of perceiving themselves is accompanied by mood swings and contradictory thoughts about themselves and others. Thus, in the course of an interview and depending on the subject or person is being addressed, patients can appear very happy and content, or very upset, disappointed, or disgusted with themselves or the therapist or other people. This is closely related to their dichotomous or all-or-nothing way of thinking, which will be described in Chapter 9.

The symptom of identity confusion is defined as a subjective feeling of uncertainty, perplexity, or conflict about identity. Patients suffering this problem feel as if they are in a constant battle about who they are and what decisions to make.

> *"I don't know who I really am. I constantly change my mind. I don't know what I like, what I need or what I want... I'm incapable of making decisions without help or going crazy in the process."*

Identity confusion is a symptom that manifests along a spectrum of severity (Steinberg, 1994), ranging from an intermittent struggle between good and bad "parts" that appear in the absence of amnesia in personality disorders (Boon & Draijer, 1991), to persistent internal fights regarding identity, characterized by constant internal dialogues, in Dissociative Identity Disorder and Unspecified Dissociative Disorder (American Psychiatric Association, 2013).

Identity confusion and alteration refer to the lack of integration of the personality, identity alteration being the most severe presentation. Within identity alteration, there can be different levels of severity, depending on whether these alternate personality states take control of the behavior and their degree of development.

> "Sometimes I lose control, I get upset, and I can't control what I do. On some occasions, I have become very aggressive... I have bits and pieces of memories of those moments, like loose parts of a movie... Then I clutch my head in my hands, I feel very embarrassed, very guilty... But I can't help it from happening again."

People with BPD often have marked changes in their mental state, in which they behave very differently. When close relatives describe them, we often hear, "*She seemed like another person.*" These changes are sometimes very extreme, patients in one state can be amnesic for what happened in the previous state, and these states configure complex behavior patterns (see chapter 8 on Dissociation). Sometimes, this fragmentation of personality is not openly displayed, but operates internally. Patients may feel as if they have different personalities or feel like puppets in the hands of reactions or impulses that they do not understand.

UNSTABLE INTERPERSONAL RELATIONSHIPS

Forming intense and unstable relationships is one of the basic criteria for BPD diagnosis. At the same time, it is one of the most vulnerable aspects in these people. A person with BPD may need other people desperately and yet feel the need to avoid this intimate contact to avoid further emotional damage. Some people carry this type of conflict into their relationships, confusing others and, finally, pushing them away.

> "I can't even understand myself... how can I expect others to understand me? I might need someone desperately one second and need them to go away the next second. After they go away I miss them but when they are close I just loose it and act crazy. It is very difficult to explain. This gets more complicated with intimate relationships because I just can't seem to make up my mind about anything."

> "Sometimes I think I am attracted to complicated people, I don't know what it is about them (or me) but I know there is something weird going on. For instance, I chose the worst possible partners for me. I end up being abused verbally and physically, but when I find a nice guy I just don't know what to do... nice guys seem to bore me. But is it really boredom? I don't think so, the truth is that they scare me. I know it doesn't make any sense! The aggressive guys should be the ones to be afraid of, but I actually feel safer with them. I know, I am a complete mess."

Some people with BPD have a disproportionate need for support, companionship, and affection, and expect others to know what they need at all times (even without saying anything). They are usually very perceptive and see other people's needs and weaknesses. However, sometimes they have difficulty observing these needs, especially when it comes to their loved ones. This sometimes leads them to use indirect methods (to idealize or devalue someone, for example) or, conversely, very direct and bold ones (suicide threats, cuts, etc.) to obtain support. This generates disturbance in family members and friends, who often perceive these behaviors as manipulative. When indirect behaviors are used, it is likely due to people with BPD not consciously admitting their need for others and, ironically, they end up pushing them away in the moments when they need them most. This tug of war often ends up with very short-lived relationships with intense beginnings and endings.

People with BPD are not aware that, in fact, this way of getting attention generates significant discomfort in others, who often feel pressured and blackmailed, and that, ultimately, these behaviors are what makes them step away.

A clear example of this behavior can be seen in the movie *Fatal Attraction*: Glenn Close plays a woman who falls in love with a man with whom she has a weekend affair. Despite knowing in advance that Michael Douglas is married, she is incapable of not following "her attraction" and gets carried away by her emotions and the intensity of the moment. So far, they both seem to agree and decide to take advantage of the opportunity (his wife is spending the weekend away and both are discrete adults). Everything looks wonderful until he wants to leave and decides to go home. It's too late ... She wants to be part of his life and he asks her to behave like an adult. She gets angry and tells him he is selfish and has not thought about her for a second.

After asking him to stay and then kicking him out of bed, when he is about to leave, she comes back with a very submissive attitude and asks him to say goodbye to her kindly, saying she "wants to be friends." He is taken aback, she kisses him, and he realizes, horrified, that she has slit her wrists. Anyway, she gets what she wants, and he stays one more night (unconsciously reinforcing her behavior). Contrary to what he is thinking, which must be something like: *"Oh, my God, what have I gotten into,"* she believes he stayed because he really cares for her.

After several encounters (always initiated by her) in which it becomes quite clear that he wants nothing to do with her, she tells him surprised: *"But why are you being so hostile, I don't want to hurt you, I love you."*

Despite his rejection, and after Michael Douglas almost chokes her during a fight, she tells him: *"Please don't leave, I'm sorry, I'll behave."* She is really just seeing what she wants to be true and ignoring all the negative parts he is showing her (in a very clear and explicit way). However, her passion blinds her and she desperately tries to get him back at any cost.

TROUBLE FUNCTIONING OR TAKING ADVANTAGE OF THEIR SKILLS

Many people with BPD are highly functional and have multiple skills that they are not able to use successfully. That is, they have the ability to achieve what they want, but their internal conflict, instability and insecurity does not allow them to exploit their potential and they end up engaging in self-sabotage.

> "I always mess everything up, I keep getting opportunities at my aunt's art gallery but I just ruin it all. I know others think I am talented, but I can't help feeling like a fraud or a phony. When I draw something for example, at first I might like it, but then I begin to think about what others might think or if it is what they expect and I end up hating it and thinking it is worthless."

This difficulty is related to many of the criteria in the *Diagnostic and Statistical Manual of Mental Disorders*, as discussed in Chapter 3.

ALTERNATING BETWEEN SUSPICIOUSNESS AND EXTREME INGENUITY

People with this disorder often act in opposite ways. Their tendency to alternate between extremes is well known. The same applies to trust. In times of stress their distrust may reach unimaginable limits, even getting close to paranoia. However, when they feel well, they can be extremely naive and completely trust the first person that comes their way. It is not uncommon for patients to bring strangers, or someone who tells them they are going through a rough patch and have nowhere to go, into their home or give them their house keys so they can go rest for a while.

> "I always do the same thing. I always think that others are like me. I go out of my way for others. I'm willing to do anything. I have even done nasty things to please others. When I meet a person who seems to be suffering, I can't help trying to end their suffering. I've taken in homeless people, people who said they were undocumented, and most of the time the results were awful. They have stolen from me, abused me, and insulted me. The worst of all is that I know I will do it again. If I find someone who is suffering and I don't help him and then it turns out to be true and no one helps them ... what hurts me most is that people take advantage of my trust and good intentions ... when they know my weak points, they always end up using them to hurt me."

This is partly related to their need to maintain intimate relationships or have friends they can trust and talk to about their problems, or simply to give others the opportunity they have not had at some point in their life when they have felt abandoned. Very often these people come to therapy after a new disappointment or scam, feeling terrible for being so "*stupid*" and "*thinking others can be like me.*"

RESORTING TO MAGICAL THINKING

Many people with BPD often use a type of magical thinking. It is like a belief in: *"I only have to have that for everything to go well."* That is, to think that a person, place, thing, behavior, or idea can make problems disappear instantly or make the person feel happy or safe. The most frequent magical thoughts are usually related to others fixing their discomfort. For instance, people with BPD may think that all they need is someone to accompany them or to whom they can give all the love they have to give, that they just have to find their best friend or the ideal partner.

The magic person may be an acquaintance, someone they connect with on a good day, a helpless person they find in the street with nowhere to go, or someone who lends them a hand in the middle of a problem. Any person, thing, or situation takes on a sort of power that is able to control their discomfort.

> Examples: *"If my ex-partner comes back to me, I'll be fine," "I just need someone to love me and heal me with their love," "If I buy another dress, I will feel better," "If I cut myself again, it will be the last time and I'll stop doing it."*

Case: *"If I had a pet, everything would be better."*

This is a patient with BPD and an animal phobia. In a group session, other participants speak of their pets and the love they give them. A few days later, she starts to think that if she had a puppy and could give it all her love and care, everything would be well. She states that with a puppy she would go for walks, which now she does not do because she has to go alone. The family does not agree, but she insists that without the pet she will not be able to improve. They finally accept. They give her a puppy and the first few days she is excited, her attention revolves around the pet and its needs (food, affection, walks, etc.).

Weeks later, she begins to feel afraid of the puppy, she feels guilty because she says the puppy is depressed because of her. She says that due to the puppy she is not eating or sleeping and if she did not have the puppy, she would feel better. She returns the pet to its former owner and weeks later starts to miss it. She says it has been a mistake and that if she had the puppy she would feel better.

In this case, the magical thinking is clear: *"I need a puppy to go for walks and feel better."* At the same time, the pet served to divert her attention from her real problem (her BPD). First her only problem is not having a dog and later the only problem is having the dog. The solution is equally magical: to have or not have it.

COMMON BELIEFS IN BPD

Besides all of the above, we can speak of variable affect, a chronic instability, impulsive behavior, self-destructive behavior, and cognitive or perception disorders at certain times of high emotion. This can lead them to feel or think in ways similar to the following:

1. **Thoughts of not being loved or being defective:** *"Nobody would love me if they knew the truth," "No one could love someone like me," "If they really knew me, they would realize how terrible I am."*

2. **Thoughts of uselessness or "not being apt for":** *"I don't know how to do anything right," "I'm a complete disaster."*

3. **Thoughts of dependency:** *"I can't depend on myself, I need someone to lean on," "If you don't come with me, I'm sure I'll fail."*

4. **Thoughts of being ignored, abandoned, or forgotten:** *"I'll be alone, no one will be there for me," "If I stop cutting myself, I'm afraid they'll forget about me," "Who could remember to call someone like me?"*

5. **Thoughts of losing control:** *"I can't control myself," "I got carried away, it's something beyond my control," "If I'm wrong, I will have messed it up completely."*

6. **Lack of self-confidence or confidence in personal decisions:** *"If I don't do what others want me to do, they'll leave me or attack me," "If I say what I really think, they'll know I'm stupid."*

7. **Distrust or suspicion in relation to other people:** *"People will hurt me, attack me, or take advantage of me," I'm sure they're being nice to me because they want something from me," "I must protect myself from others."*

8. **Fear of being overwhelmed, deceived, or betrayed by their emotions:** *"I must control my emotions or something terrible will happen," "I can't show how glad I was to see him, or he won't come back," "If she knows what I'm really feeling, she'll think I'm crazy."*

9. **Self-punishment or self-sabotage:** *"I'm a bad person, I deserve to be punished," "If I am so unhappy, it's because I deserve it," "I can only find one explanation to this discomfort: I provoke it myself; therefore, I deserve to suffer."*

It is normal for beliefs like these and their corresponding ways of thinking to lead these people to feeling vulnerable and disabled in the world. Thus, they act as if they were in a constant battle with the world, themselves, and other people. The belief of not fitting in leads them to look continuously for their place in a world that is perceived as dangerous, full of unexpected things and people who are ready to hurt them and will not allow them the slightest mistake.

Fig. 1: The big eye in the sky on the left is saying, "You're useless." The one on the right is laughing. The black cloud represents the patient's sensation of being doomed.

Such ingrained beliefs can be understood very well from the adaptive information processing (AIP) model that is the basis for EMDR (Shapiro, 1989, 2001). The AIP model proposes that images, thoughts, emotions, and physical sensations associated with a traumatic event or events are dysfunctionally stored in the brain and become entrenched beliefs and schemes that are difficult to change. Other therapies, such as Schema Therapy (Young, 1994) and Cognitive Analytic Therapy (Ryle & Kerr, 2002), speak of rigid ways of functioning that are generated early, but persist almost unmodified into adulthood. These schema and patterns are difficult to change without specific interventions. For more information about this see Chapter 15 on psychotherapies.

In the next chapter we will delve into each of the diagnostic criteria of BPD. Then we will go beyond the clinical presentation to understand the *roots* and the possible origin of the symptoms.

Chapter 3
Borderline Personality Disorder: Understanding DSM Criteria

INTRODUCTION

Clinicians use a book called DSM (*Diagnostic and Statistical Manual of Mental Disorders*) to establish mental health diagnoses. Borderline personality disorder (BPD) is one of the many diagnoses listed in the DSM-5 (the latest version of this manual). This manual has a format that seeks to organize and communicate clinical information, capture the complexity of clinical situations, and describe the heterogeneity of individuals with the same diagnosis. BPD is located in this manual, under the category of personality disorders.

A personality disorder is a permanent and inflexible pattern of inner experience and behavior that markedly deviates from the expectations of the individual's culture, has its onset in adolescence or early adulthood, is stable over time, and involves discomfort or damage to the individual (American Psychiatric Association, 1996)

The DSM-5 describes ten personality disorders, which, are divided into three groups (A, B, and C) based on similar characteristics. Group A includes paranoid, schizoid, and schizotypal personality disorders, which often appear odd or eccentric; group B includes antisocial, borderline, histrionic, and narcissistic personality disorders, which are often perceived as dramatic, emotional, or unstable; group C includes avoidant, dependent, and obsessive-compulsive personality disorders, which are typically described as anxious or fearful.

BPD is located within group B and is defined as a pervasive pattern of instability in interpersonal relationships, self-image, and affects, with marked impulsivity beginning in early adulthood (adolescence) and present in a variety of contexts. The DSM-5 contains a list of nine items called diagnostic criteria, which we will explore in depth in point 3 of this chapter.

The purpose of this chapter is to reflect on the BPD concept/diagnosis from a clinical perspective and to explain the relationship between the diagnostic criteria in the DSM-5. Although in the manual they are listed independently, in practice this independence is relative. Moreover, addressing these criteria (which translate into difficulties) independently can be one of the factors that contribute to confusion and hinder the understanding of this disorder.

BRIEF HISTORY

The borderline description has been considered a catchall for many years and used when a clinician was not sure of the patient's diagnosis. The term borderline emerged along these lines and professionals resorted to it when it was not clear whether the patient was suffering from neurosis (mildly ill patients) or psychosis (very ill patients). The idea of using this term came from the difficulties observed in a group of patients who did not fit in any of the two poles of disease and who seemed to oscillate between characteristics of normal functioning and characteristics of pathological functioning, thus placing themselves in the boundary between normality and pathology. Currently, the borderline diagnosis is conceived as an advanced and potentially severe level of maladaptive functioning of the personality. It signifies a habitual level of performance and a lasting pattern of altered functioning (Millon & Davis, 1998) that, although it can be stabilized for a considerable period of time and give the appearance of an adaptive functioning, persists over time causing significant limitations in the quality of life of people who suffer from it.

Although the term borderline goes back to the middle of the last century, BPD was not formally recognized as a diagnosis until 1980 (Cervera, Haro, & Martinez-Raga, 2005). Since its emergence as an official diagnosis in the DSM-III (1980), there has been much research and it has generated great controversy among professionals, particularly around treatment and possible prognosis as discussed in chapter 1.

BPD is the most common personality disorder in clinical populations. According to Selva, Bellver, and Carabal (2005), this is due to its high comorbidity with affective disorders, anxiety, and substance abuse, and the high rate of suicide attempts, which all together cause great demand for care from these patients.

According to the DSM-5, this disorder occurs in 2% of the population. Most authors estimate a prevalence of between 1 and 2%, but others consider that these figures fall short and that, in fact, prevalence would be around 4% of the population. BPD is more common in females, with a ratio between 2:1 and 4:1, although this could be due to bias in the sample selection and to women seeking treatment more often than men (Cervera et al., 2005). Another bias may be due to cultural factors. Expressing of emotions is more acceptable in women, so men tend to hide suffering and handle it in very different ways. So, while it is common (and expected) for women to express their emotions intensely and tend toward self-directed aggression, i.e., harming themselves (self-aggressiveness), men tend to repress the expression of emotions and direct their aggression outwardly (hetero-aggressiveness). One of the cultural reasons is that the expression of emotions by men is often associated with weakness. These comments are based on clinical experience and are intended to invite reflection, although there are many exceptions and, therefore, this cannot be generalized.

BPD is a complex and heterogeneous syndrome that stems from the need to categorize a group of patients with emotional instability and impulse control disorders that do not fit within the traditional syndromes (Cervera et al., 2005). It is a diagnosis that in itself explains nothing, because the reality is that a person can get this label in many different ways. That is, the diagnosis continues to be a description of a set of problems that some people have, which are grouped and then divided into categories, depending on similarities. For all these reasons, it is interesting to delve into the diagnostic criteria and the relationship that may exist between them.

THE *DIAGNOSTIC AND STATISTIC MANUAL OF MENTAL DISORDERS* DIAGNOSTIC CRITERIA

DESCRIPTION AND INTERRELATION

As mentioned in the introduction to this chapter, clinicians use a book called *DSM* to make mental health diagnoses. According to the DSM-5, the latest version of the manual, the essential feature of BPD is a pervasive pattern of instability in interpersonal relationships, self-image, and affects, with marked impulsivity beginning by early adulthood (adolescence) and present in a variety of contexts. While this is true and describes some of the features or difficulties of people who receive this diagnosis, it is not very enlightening for the lay reader or even for professionals lacking experience in this field. The DSM-5 contains a list of nine items called diagnostic criteria, which are transcribed below. In order to establish a diagnosis of BPD, the clinician should observe the presence of five of these nine items:

1. Frantic efforts to avoid real or imagined abandonment.

2. Pattern of unstable and intense interpersonal relationships characterized by alternating between extremes of idealization and devaluation.

3. Identity disturbance: markedly and persistently unstable self-image or sense of self.

4. Impulsivity in at least two areas that are potentially self-damaging (i.e.: spending, sex, substance abuse, reckless driving, binge eating...)

5. Recurrent suicidal behavior, gestures, or threats, or self-mutilating behavior.

6. Affective instability due to a marked reactivity of mood (e.g.: intense episodic dysphoria, irritability or anxiety, usually lasting a few hours and only rarely more than a few days).

7. Chronic feelings of emptiness.

8. Inappropriate, intense anger or difficulty controlling anger (e.g.: frequent displays of temper, constant anger, recurrent physical fights).

9. Transient, stress-related paranoid ideation or severe dissociative symptoms.

The only requirements that the DSM indicates, in addition to meeting at least five of the diagnostic criteria reflected on this list, are that the characteristics are long-term (years), persistent, and intense, and interfere significantly in the person's quality of life.

Simply transcribing the DSM diagnostic criteria to describe BPD in this chapter would not clarify too much, since trying to define and clarify a personality disorder through a list of specific symptoms is quite difficult. For this reason, it would be interesting to reflect and elaborate on each of these criteria, in addition to exposing other features usually manifested in people with this diagnosis, which do not appear in the aforementioned manual. As these criteria are interrelated, we could say that one feature feeds or activates another; examples are presented to facilitate the understanding of this interrelationship.

CRITERION 1 - FRANTIC EFFORTS TO AVOID REAL OR IMAGINED ABANDONMENT

Many people with BPD claim to suffer badly when they are alone, even for very short periods of time. Others state that they feel lonely even when surrounded by people. This fear makes them particularly vulnerable to abandonment and encourages the activation of alert signals when faced with relational stimuli or situations perceived as threatening. Feeling rejected or ignored may trigger very intense emotional reactions in the patient. While anyone may feel very uncomfortable when they fear being abandoned and may react in different ways to loss, it is rare that these reactions reach the extremes manifested by people with BPD.

Let us see how these factors interrelate and feed each other with a common example. A patient thinks that her partner is going to leave her. Although she has no evidence that this is true, she ends up convincing herself of it and reacts by threatening: *"If you leave me, I'll kill myself,"* begging: *"Please don't leave me, I'll be good,"* or by destructive behaviors and self-harm (let us say that criterion 5 of intense suicidal behaviors or threats would be triggered). This same patient may resort to compensatory and/or evasive behaviors, such as drinking, taking drugs, or self-medicating in order to *"sleep and not think,"* and she may even sleep with one or more people she has met recently just to feel connected to someone (criterion 4 of impulsivity would become activated in at least two areas that are potentially self-damaging). Another common response, also associated with criterion 4, is resorting to impulsive and risky behaviors (such as driving recklessly without thinking about the consequences, spending more money than she has, or betting on things she does not own).

Some authors consider that people with BPD need a support figure who allows them to contain their anxieties and place themselves in the world with some confidence. This would explain the difficulties that many people with this diagnosis experience when they perceive the threat (real or imagined) of losing an important figure. Kernberg et al. (2008) speak of a very intense fear of abandonment that is due to the inability of people with BPD to develop an inner sense of other people that is consistent and permanent.

Criterion 1 is related to the sense of learned helplessness and attachment issues, especially insecure attachments as described by Bowlby (1969, 1973, 1980) with the tendency to depend on others.

In their first therapy sessions, patients often report that they feel *"very dependent."* This dependence can manifest in many different ways. The most common is what partners and families describe as clingy and dependent. However, we can also find more complex manifestations accompanied by defenses, which can be expressed indirectly, such as with contempt or attempts to control manifested in many different ways (sometimes from a seemingly weaker position, other times with threats...).

The behaviors that emerge from criterion 1 can lead to confusion in clinical assessments. When people with BPD are faced with the possibility of being abandoned, their fragility, their feelings of dependence, and their tendency to act desperately to keep people at their side can lead some clinicians think of a diagnosis of dependent personality disorder. In this regard, it is interesting to note that these intense manifestations are simply a clear example of the complexity of BPD.

CRITERION 2. PATTERN OF UNSTABLE AND INTENSE INTERPERSONAL RELATIONSHIPS CHARACTERIZED BY ALTERNATING BETWEEN EXTREMES OF IDEALIZATION AND DEVALUATION

Criterion 1 (frantic efforts to avoid real or imagined abandonment), describes how it is common for people with this diagnosis to feel dependent and that sometimes this dependence is manifested indirectly (e.g., hostile responses toward others). Due to this, their ways of interacting cause great confusion in people they relate to and leads to highly variable and often conflicting relationships.

It is very difficult to understand that *"leave me alone, I never want to see you again"* really means *"please don't leave me, I need you."* Patients are not always aware of this lack of connection between what they feel and need, and what they do and/or say, so they end up puzzled by other people's reactions and viceversa (a key aspect when working in therapy sessions).

People with BPD may idealize those who care for them or anyone they just met (especially when they perceive a special connection or when they feel appreciated, heard, and/or valued). However, this usually changes rapidly and can switch from idealization to devaluation when they think they are not paid enough attention or they are not loved and are rejected. Any little thing can trigger a deep sense of betrayal and pain. Besides being related to criterion 1 (fear of abandonment) and criterion 6 (affective instability due to a marked reactivity of mood), this is also related to another aspect: low tolerance for frustration and great difficulty channeling it properly. Although low tolerance for frustration does not appear reflected as a diagnostic criterion, it is a common feature mentioned by patients, families, and professionals.

Other factors that can trigger changes in perception of others include: extreme insecurity felt by many people with this diagnosis, hypersensitivity, and cognitive distortions. Many feel like frauds and strive to maintain a façade of apparent normality (another aspect that baffles observers). Hypersensitivity may make them appear alert to any possible warning sign involving rejection or the possibility of being truly known (since it is usual for them to believe that if others get to know them, they will turn away). Once again, the relationship to criterion 1 (frantic efforts to avoid real or imagined abandonment) becomes clear.

Another aspect that complicates interpersonal relationships for people with this diagnosis is the tendency to personalize the reactions and/or comments of others and interpret them as something against them. Sometimes, when they are very emotionally activated (criterion 6) they can get really suspicious and may even think (and believe) that others want to harm them, distorting reality (criterion 9). This is related to cognitive distortions, as they can interpret what others are doing in terms of what they think or feel.

This criterion is related to difficulty learning from experience (from mistakes, successes, etc.), lack of skills, lack of supportive interpersonal experiences, and invalidating environments. It could also be related to attachment problems, identity alteration, tendency to measure their worth in terms of what others think, and even, in some cases, dissociative symptomatology.

CRITERION 3. IDENTITY DISTURBANCE: MARKEDLY AND PERSISTENTLY UNSTABLE SELF-IMAGE OR SENSE OF SELF

Overall, identity is a set of features that allow us to have a sense of who we are, what we want, and where we are going.

According to Novella and Plumed (2005), a healthy identity includes the ability to choose an appropriate path at an occupational level, reach intimacy with others, and find a place in society. The opposite pole of identity would be identity confusion, which Erikson (1980) originally referred to as identity diffusion and which can manifest itself in a variety of ways: subjective feeling of incoherence, difficulty assuming roles and occupational choices, or tendency to confuse their own attributes, emotions, and desires in intimate relationships with those of the other person, thus fearing loss of personal identity when a relationship ends (Cervera et al., 2005).

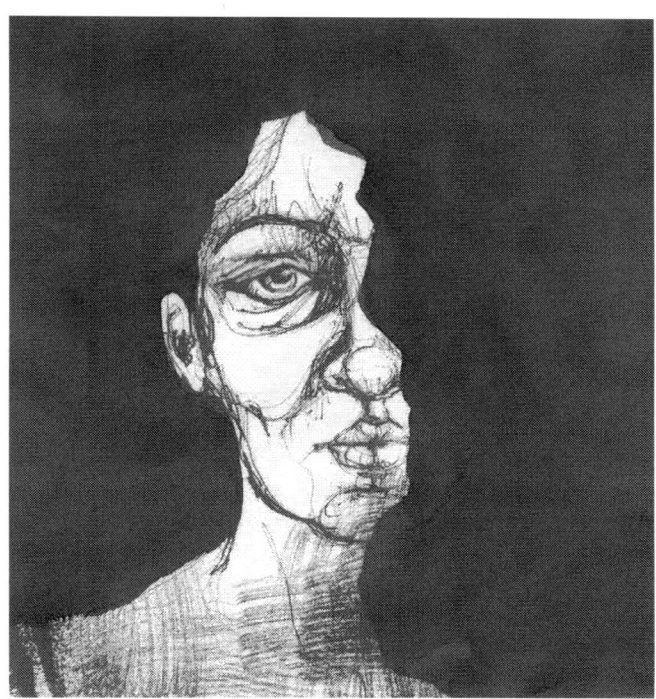

Often, people with BPD indicate not knowing how they feel, what they like, or what they want to do. Some say they get bored easily and are always looking for something to do.

Others describe a feeling of emptiness that they are unable to fill with anything (criterion 7), which can lead them to engaging in many projects and goals that are difficult to attain and running into multiple complications when prioritizing and getting organized.

As mentioned previously, when people do not have a distinct identity and cannot find an explanation for what is happening to them, they often search for clues in others: something that allows them to explain their confusion and uncertainty, an explanation that can decrease their guilt and, in turn, allow others to understand them. As discussed in Chapter 1, this is also related to one of the many aspects that are observed during hospitalizations: mimetization. Often, during hospitalizations, people with diffuse identities may take the group of patients in their psychiatric unit as a reference and start copying and manifesting these people's symptoms, coming to see them as their own.

Many people with BPD indicate difficulties in finding their path or finding out who they are, and are overwhelmed when they have to answer basic questions like: *"How would you describe yourself?"* or *"What do you like to do?"*

It is often said that people with BPD are impatient and have great difficulty being consistent with their goals. This lack of perseverance is related to identity disturbance and the tendency to do what is expected of them, rather than thinking and reflecting on what they would want to do. They often show confusion and variability around their values and these may vary according to the opinions or preferences of the people with whom they interact.

It is common for people with this diagnosis to feel like frauds and adopt a façade of apparent normality. They often try to please (especially strangers), put on masks, and act according to what they think is expected of them. It is also common for them to draw masks, represent themselves as clowns or phonies as we can see in figure 2.

Fig 2: "I feel like a clown who always plays to the gallery. I have to be okay in order not to have any problems with others; I cannot express the reality of what I feel because they will not understand."

Helen Deutsch (1986) described a group of patients, she called *as if personalities,* who tended to adopt other people's characteristics in order to retain their love. According to this author, these patients did not have a well-defined self, so they resorted to this complex way of keeping others inside of them. Robert Knight (1986) described a group of patients who, in favorable conditions, could appear superficially adapted.

According to Sanjuan, Moltó, & Rivero (2005), some of the symptoms of patients with BPD are similar to those experienced by patients with PTSD. In this sense, identity alteration could be understood as dissociative phenomena (Cervera et al., 2005). Patients who have suffered abuse, for example, may react impulsively to stimuli that remind them of or make them relive the trauma.

This would turn into marked reactivity, mood changes, and, in some cases, especially when it is severe and prolonged abuse, the manifestation of dissociative reactions or extreme suspiciousness.

This criterion, like the previous two, is related to attachment issues, lack of stable models, and the tendency to measure their worth in terms of what others think. In addition, identity alteration is frequently related to dissociative symptoms. The latter would explain many of the apparently unpredictable and disconnected reactions and that can be seen in many people with BPD.

CRITERION 4. IMPULSIVITY IN AT LEAST TWO AREAS THAT ARE POTENTIALLY SELF-DAMAGING (I.E.: SPENDING, SEX, SUBSTANCE ABUSE, RECKLESS DRIVING, BINGE EATING…)

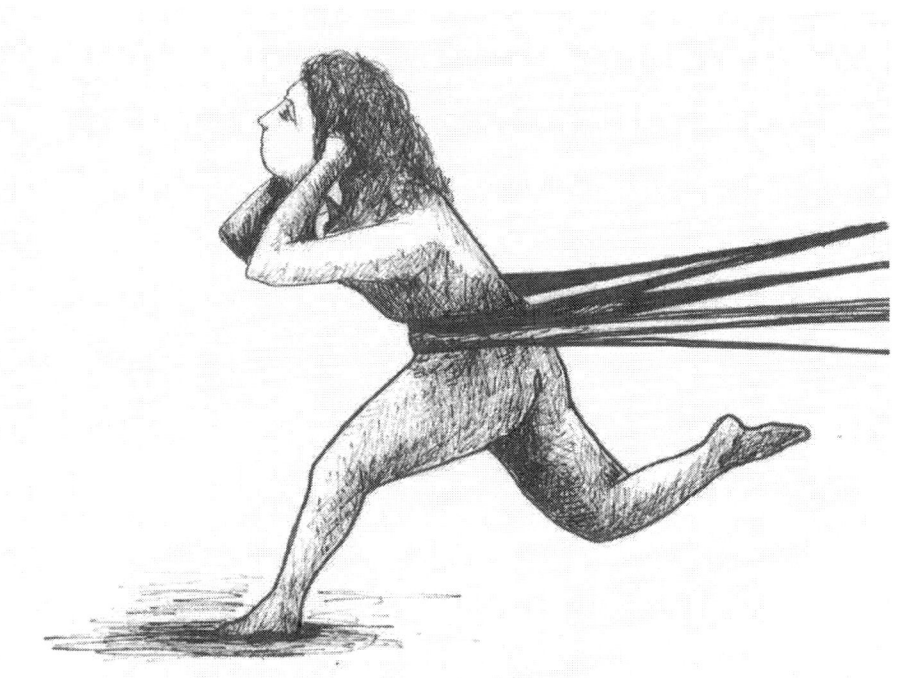

People with this diagnosis often perceive and describe themselves as impulsive, but it is unusual for them to think about why they behave or react impulsively. They often say things like *"I'm like this, I can't help it"* and come to believe that they have no control over their behavior. While this may be true at certain times, it is also true that many impulsive reactions could be replaced with more adaptive ones. This will not happen spontaneously and, of course, it will not happen without practice, but it can be achieved with psychoeducation and reflection exercises that help the person identify their impulsive tendencies and think of alternatives.

The most common examples of impulsive behaviors are those mentioned in this DSM criterion: tendency to splurge (even more than they can afford), substance abuse (although often in order to disconnect, to not think, not just for pleasure), reckless driving (usually in order to regulate a difficult-to-tolerate emotional state), and binge eating (due to anxiety, as a compensatory measure, as a way to regulate emotions). The key difference among impulsive behaviors is the motivation that leads people to react in that way. Someone may binge on food because they want to eat and they do not necessarily feel bad. This would not be the case in a person with BPD, in whom the bingeing behavior would have a regulatory function. People may take drugs or drink alcohol because they like it, because they like the feeling, but not necessarily because of intense discomfort they desperately need to stop (which would be what usually makes a person with this diagnosis abuse substances).

Shapiro (1965) defined impulsivity as the tendency to act, after a momentary stimulus, without a previous plan or without a clear direction or desire (Cervera et al., 2005). This defines exactly what many patients feel and indicate when they say that they don't know why they reacted that way. Here is one example: a patient receives some news that baffles him and affects him (trigger). Following this, many reactions can be activated: one patient can get in his car and drive recklessly, another one may make obsessive phone calls, and a third one may take drugs or whatever else helps him better tolerate his emotional state. Patients will do all of this without stopping to think about possible consequences or actually being aware of what triggered them in the first place. If the main emotion activated is anger, there could be a cumulative effect between this criterion and number 8 (inappropriate anger or difficulties controlling anger), which would multiply impulsive reactions (whether biological or learned).

Lack of skills to regulate emotions can trigger criterion 1 factors (frantic efforts to avoid real or imagined abandonment), criterion 5 factors (intense behaviors, suicidal threats, or self-mutilating behavior), and criterion 6 factors (affective instability due to a marked reactivity of mood). All this, in turn, can activate this criterion in particular (impulsivity in at least two potentially dangerous areas). Considering the link between impulsivity, some suicide attempts and actually committing suicide, an interrelationship between criteria 4 (impulsivity in at least two areas that are potentially self-damaging) and 5 (intense behaviors, recurrent suicidal threats, or self-mutilating behaviors) can also often be found.

Although impulsivity (criterion 4) can have a significant biological basis, it is also related to difficulty in learning from experience, low tolerance for frustration, difficulty reflecting on the possible consequences, hypersensitivity, and abrupt mood swings. All this translates into a lack of skills and resources, which makes people with BPD vulnerable and reactive.

This criterion, like the previous two, can at times become activated in relationship to dissociative symptoms. The person may have blocked certain memories that can be activated by disturbing news in an apparently unconnected way, which can access a certain unconscious emotional part of them.

CRITERION 5. RECURRENT SUICIDAL BEHAVIOR, GESTURES, OR THREATS, OR SELF-MUTILATING BEHAVIOR

This criterion encompasses many of the reactions for which BPD patients come to the ER or are hospitalized.

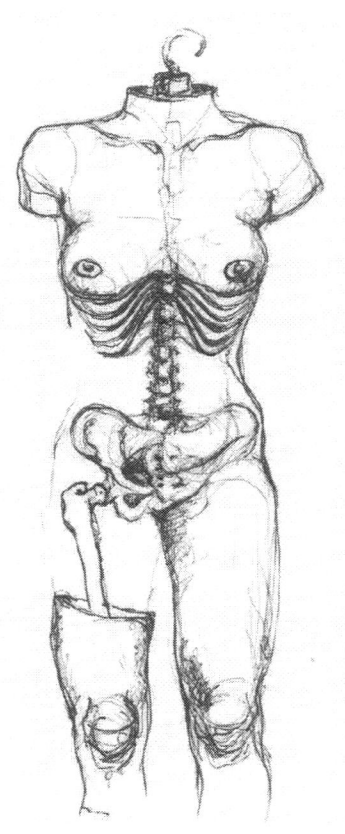

In order to understand this criterion, we must understand the triggers – the motivation behind the apparently maladaptive behavior. Intense behaviors, suicidal threats, and self-destructive behaviors such as self-mutilation are often interpreted as blackmail and manipulation when, in fact, in most cases, they are the way the patient has found to effectively cope with difficult emotions and to calm down.

People with this diagnosis are known to have hypersensitivity and tremendous difficulty tolerating and managing negative emotions. When people have not acquired the expected kinds of resources to cope with unforeseen complications, manage difficulties, and resolve conflicts, it is common for them to find their own way to regulate themselves.

Cuts, burns, suicide threats, and even suicide attempts are often the only way they find to cope with difficulties. For many patients, these behaviors are adaptive and effective and, at times, are what helps them stay alive. Behind many suicide attempts, we find a desire to live, not to die. In most cases, if we explore the reasons that led them to attempt suicide, we find information that indicates that the person wants to stop suffering and learn to live differently.

For some authors, BPD is the equivalent of suicidal personality and this makes sense when we consider that many studies set the rate of completed suicides at around 10% and the rate of suicide attempts around 70%. Researchers, who studied the prevalence of personality disorders in representative samples of patients admitted after self-destructive acts, found BPD to be the primary diagnosis in up to 55% of subjects (Cervera, Haro, & Martinez-Raga, 2005; Soderberg, 2001).

People who fear being abandoned can learn to relate through threats and even think that suicide is the only way out of a situation (especially when they think that everyone is just tired of them and this is confirmed by a new abandonment). The pattern of unstable relationships can make people with this diagnosis resort to self-harm or threats as a way to communicate and interact with others. In addition, the abrupt change in a relationship, especially when they go from idealization to devaluation or disappointment, can trigger intense feelings of despair that may activate feelings of emptiness, which in turn will trigger intense reactions, including suicidal threats or self-injurious behaviors.

Impulsivity and self-harming behaviors are frequently related to difficulty learning from experience and lack of skills. It would also be related to difficulty tolerating discomfort, self-soothing, regulating emotions, and seeing other ways out of suffering. And in some cases, we will also find a relationship with dissociative symptoms. These behaviors could be explained within the procedures used by self-states (the observed behaviors can represent the performance of different roles, e.g., self-punishing and abusive roles toward oneself).

CRITERION 6. AFFECTIVE INSTABILITY DUE TO A MARKED REACTIVITY OF MOOD (E.G.:INTENSE EPISODIC DYSPHORIA, IRRITABILITY OR ANXIETY, USUALLY LASTING A FEW HOURS AND ONLY RARELY MORE THAN A FEW DAYS)

People with BPD often present emotional instability that affects many areas and can manifest with abrupt mood changes. The basic dysphoric mood (i.e., the tendency to feel sad or discouraged) is often interrupted by periods of anger, distress, or despair, and it is unusual for a state of wellbeing or satisfaction to take over.

The perception of something threatening can make people change their minds in radical ways and that, affected by emotional arousal, they may present with abrupt changes in mood, feelings, and/or behavior. For example, a person with BPD may shift from thinking that her partner misbehaves with her and is not good for her to thinking that she could not live without him, when faced with the threat or the idea of being alone. With these intense, black-or-white feelings or thoughts, disappointment often turns into anger, which can be either directed towards others, in the form of verbal or physical abuse, or toward oneself as suicide attempts or self-harming behaviors.

According to Novella and Plumed (2005), the frequent presence of dysphoric states or intense anger in these patients can be seen from the perspective of their fragile identity, which would explain the interrelationship of this criterion with criterion 3 (identity alteration). People who meet this criterion are especially vulnerable to external factors. In this sense, it is interesting to mention Linehan (1993a), who believes that people with this diagnosis are overly sensitive to emotional stimuli and have very intense reactions even to low stimuli. For Linehan, this criterion seems to represent the foundation of the disorder.

Although affective instability might have a greater biological basis in some cases, and therefore, better response to drug treatments, we cannot ignore that reactive tendencies observed in most people with this diagnosis are usually related to external and relational factors. That is, the weight of parenting, learning, and life experience are aspects that must be taken into account. Like suicide attempts and self-injury, affective instability can be triggered at any time by dissociated emotions, memories, and experiences that may manifest in an extreme way depending on role and experience.

CRITERION 7. CHRONIC FEELINGS OF EMPTINESS

Some patients describe the feeling of emptiness as a very intense feeling that invades their whole being; others state that there is nothing that fulfills them or has meaning, or speak of a pain that pierces them and destroys them. Others describe it as a bottomless well filled up with anguish (Mosquera 2007, 2010).

Many people with this diagnosis get bored easily and are always trying to find something to do, which sometimes leads to high risk activities or behaviors, since intense emotions can make them feel alive. This often desperate search is a way to give meaning to life and to try to fill a void they describe as brutal, bleak, and impossible to fill.

Most patients with feelings of emptiness speak of their need to mitigate those feelings and of desperate attempts to fill up that emptiness. For many, a common way to handle these overwhelming feelings is to resort to harmful behaviors with the intention of disconnecting (criterion 4), even to the point of self-harm and, in some cases, suicide attempts (criterion 5).

These feelings of emptiness make them feel incomplete and affect the images they have of themselves and others. They often idealize other people because they imagine that their lives are fuller and more deserving of living than theirs.

In addition to the above, at times this sense of emptiness makes them feel very dependent on others (many feel that only others can fill that void).

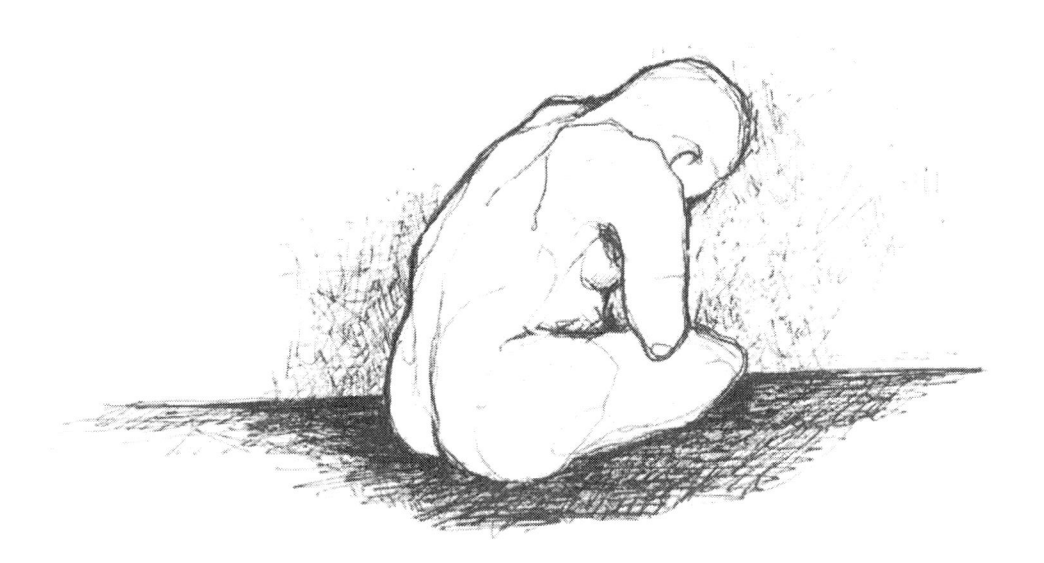

In these cases, the interaction with criterion 1 (frantic efforts to avoid real or imagined abandonment) is obvious. When people need others to feel more full or less empty, they place themselves in a vulnerable position, because they depend on external factors to feel better. This would explain the disproportionate reactions that can be observed in some patients when they fear being abandoned (criterion 1) and the fragile identity (criterion 3) they need to capture, while at the same time needing to absorb and feed on the qualities they observe in others to feel that they really exist and/or are somebody.

This criterion is related to both avoidant and ambivalent attachment styles that may make people feel very empty during times when relational difficulties and problems in regulating their emotions manifest.

CRITERION 8. INAPPROPRIATE, INTENSE ANGER OR DIFFICULTY CONTROLLING ANGER (E.G.: FREQUENT DISPLAYS OF TEMPER, CONSTANT ANGER, RECURRENT PHYSICAL FIGHTS)

Some people with BPD have unpredictable responses, consisting of abrupt mood changes or sudden emotional outbursts. These explosions can be verbal, physical, or both. In some cases there can be a tendency to switch between different types of explosion.

Angry outbursts can be frightening. People may give the impression of being totally out of control, shaken, acting on impulses, and disregarding the consequences of their behavior. The reality is that during such outburst they cannot help themselves, although they may often be aware that what they are doing will push people away even more. When they get angry with someone, it is as if that someone ceases to be a person with feelings and becomes the object of their hatred and cause of their discomfort: the enemy.

Although some people with this diagnosis can be emotionally and even physically abusive, it is important to understand that, usually, they do not try to harm anyone. Often, what happens is that a primary emotion (fear, for example) turns into a secondary emotion (shame for having been afraid). Because they lack more adaptive coping skills, they end up using defense mechanisms, which they are often not even aware of using and need to learn to identify in order to start generating changes. Sometimes, behind these incomprehensible reactions, we find fear of abandonment (related to criterion 1), a search for acceptance or interest (sometimes the affected person is trying to have the other person reassure them and tell them they will be there, that they will not be abandoned), and sometimes difficulties relating to others in a satisfactory way (criterion 2, unstable and intense interpersonal relationships).

People with BPD are known to act impulsively, without thinking about the consequences of their actions. Some are moved by the desire or the intensity of the moment, the excitement of the situation, or the possible immediate reward or gratification. Others are moved by true desperation, anxiety, and feeling unable to stop once they've taken action. Sometimes they realize what they are doing and this is even more frustrating. An example would be: *"I knew I was screwing up big time, I saw it in his eyes, I knew he was scared and would not want to see me again, but I could not stop; being aware of that triggered me even more."* This would be a clear example of difficulty tolerating emotions and regulating them effectively.

Expressions of anger may be followed by sorrow, remorse, and guilt and contribute to the beliefs they have of being bad, out of control, selfish, or freaks.

It is noteworthy that anger interferes with logic but is more bearable than fear: it makes them feel less vulnerable. When people are angry, we cannot expect them to act with logic, not because they do not want to, but because they cannot. Simple irritation can manifest in such an intense way that is difficult to distinguish between anger and a critical situation. In fact, at times, simple irritation may end up as an uncontrolled crisis in which both the affected person and their family or anyone present has forgotten why the discussion started.

Considering that the purpose of suicide attempts is diverse and, at times, intended to express anger or to feel free from overwhelming emotions, we will find an interrelation between criteria 5 (intense behaviors, suicidal threats or self-injurious behaviors), 6 (affective instability due to a marked reactivity of mood), and 8 (inappropriate anger or difficulty controlling it). If, in addition to this, we consider that impulsive aggression may be one of the factors that increase the risk of suicidal behavior in patients with BPD, this relationship intensifies.

Intense anger and inability to manage angry outburst are related to lack of skills and positive interpersonal experiences, parenting styles, and learning, since it is common for people with this diagnosis to have serious problems regulating their emotional states and soothing themselves. In addition, they are often used to defending themselves as a strategy of endurance, and even of survival. In some specific cases, dissociative symptoms may explain many of the reactions of inappropriate anger, because a certain emotional experience can connect with similar previous experiences and activate the response mode learned at an earlier age.

CRITERION 9. TRANSIENT, STRESS-RELATED PARANOID IDEATION OR SEVERE DISSOCIATIVE SYMPTOMS

Many people with BPD are extremely vulnerable and sensitive. Some authors speak of difficulties regulating emotional states and hypersensitivity to stimuli in general. This would explain the suspicion that can be observed in people with BPD when they are emotionally activated. At times of high stress, they may think that others want to hurt them and become extremely suspicious.

Anecdotally, we can mention that many patients draw an eye to describe the feeling of being watched and judged at all times. Transient paranoid ideation often generates confusion among professionals and can lead to inaccurate diagnoses, especially with group A personality disorders (paranoid, schizoid, and schizotypal).

Severe dissociative symptoms are often related to early experiences and are often found in patients who have been neglected and abused in childhood.

This criterion is key because it could explain many of the seemingly unpredictable and disproportionate reactions of people with this diagnosis, especially in cases where the person has suffered abuse or neglect.

Are DSM criteria useful?

The DSM criteria discussed throughout this chapter are based on trait dimensions (patterns of behavior, emotion, and cognition that characterize people). In this regard, it is interesting to to keep in mind Beck, Freemans, and David's (1990) point of view that personality traits are not pathological in themselves; they may be adaptive or maladaptive, under different circumstances. It is true that aspects of some criteria can be seen in the general population and that these do not necessarily indicate the presence of pathology. However, it is rare for one person to manifest five of the BPD criteria without experiencing serious difficulties in daily functioning. In order to consider each of the criteria as significant and indicative of the presence of borderline pathology, these are not to be isolated or occasional (if this were so, the diagnosis would be wrong). Rather, it is the simultaneous observation and interrelated functioning of all these maladaptive factors that characterizes those with BPD.

The DSM classification has been useful in unifying criteria and provides a common language, but it often ignores the pathological richness of this disorder. The genesis of BPD is the coming together of various genetic, biochemical, neurophysiological factors and circumstances, along with others that are learned, transmitted, and modulated in a dynamic way from childhood to adulthood (Rubio Larrosa, 2006).

As mentioned in section 1 of this chapter, according to the DSM-5, the general criteria for diagnosing personality disorders require the presence of an enduring pattern of inner experience and behavior that deviates markedly from the expectations of culture, and the affective, cognitive, interpersonal activity, and impulse control of each person. The pattern must be inflexible and persistent, cover a wide range of personal and social situations, and cause clinically significant distress or impairment in social, occupational, or other important areas of an individual's activity. Finally, the pattern must be stable and long-term, and its onset must be traced back at least to adolescence or early adulthood.

This chapter cannot be complete without referring to the possible causes or triggers of BPD, since it is another issue that has generated and still generates controversy. Regarding this, the contributions of Linehan (2003a) on emotional dysregulation and disabling environment, and Fonagy's (2000) proposals, which include Gunderson's (2002) ideas and descriptions on the importance of attachment in people with BPD should be highlighted. Joel Paris (1994) indicates that chemical imbalances, psychological adversity, and environment conflicts by themselves do not explain the occurrence of psychopathology. He indicates that, in the etiology of any mental disorder, numerous interactions of biological, psychological, and social factors are involved. Paris (1994) uses the diathesis-stress model of Monroe and Simons (1991) (a general theory of non-reductionist and interactional psychopathology) in order to explain that each of the categories of mental disorders is associated with some kind of genetic vulnerability and to conceptualize the way in which predisposition and stressors interact and shape personality disorders. He explains that genes themselves are not the direct cause of mental disorders, but they shape individual variability in the form of temperament and traits.

For Paris (1994), some of these variations in temperament are a vulnerability to psychopathology, though he says that, in general, features only become maladaptive under specific environmental conditions. In other words, predisposition becomes apparent when exposed to stressors. There is a two-way interaction between predisposition and stressors: genetic variability influences the way individuals respond to the environment, while environmental factors determine the expression of genes. These relationships would help explain why life events do not always cause pathological consequences.

In connection with the above, it is interesting to note that personality is not only what makes each person be him or herself, but what makes each person different from other people. Individuality is the result of a unique history of transactions between biological and contextual factors, and each personality is a unique product, so it cannot be understood by applying universal laws. Due to this, the understanding of personality requires an approach based on development that is as rich, from a descriptive point of view, as the history of the person; so rich that, in fact, could only be called biographical (Millon & Davis, 1998).

Currently, BPD remains controversial and there is not unanimity on where it would be best located within clinical manuals. Although the purpose of this chapter is not an exhaustive analysis of BPD and its adequate diagnostic location, it is interesting to note that the divergent points of view on this issue reflect the complexity and variability of the clinical picture. For Zanarini (1993), for example, it should be located in the section on impulse disorders, for Kroll (1998) and others it should be located with the post-traumatic stress disorders, and for Akiskal (1981) within the affective disorders. From the author's point of view, personality disorders represent a separate entity and BPD should have its own specific category within the personality disorders spectrum.

In short, BPD is a disorder in which emotional instability, high reactivity to external factors, an almost permanent feeling of vulnerability, and great difficulty functioning in an adaptive or effective way for long periods of time prevail. Most people with BPD lead chaotic lives and have the experience of not fitting in society. This is observed and reflected in the many difficulties that manifest in their relationships with others, in their view of events and of the environment, and their variable and fragile self-concept as we will see in the following chapter about the patient's perspective.

Chapter 4
Borderline Personality Disorder from the Point of View of Patients

"I'm like a doped-up rookie tightrope walker who sets up hurdles for herself, who puts so much pressure on herself like someone putting salt on an open wound. I feel that everyone is going to judge me all the time for everything I do and don't do. On one side are my loved ones, worried, watching that I don't take steps back, that I get better. On the other side, the rest of the people, mute witnesses, people who I think look at my suffering with curiosity and don't get involved, they're just waiting ... In the middle, the starry star that I am, ready to walk the tightrope, which, of course, I've smeared with Vaseline. Always complicating things, I decide to walk the rope without a net, to atone for my sins in front of those who love me and scream at the others that I'm still alive. Who would stand this pressure?

"But I don't really throw myself, I just take a couple steps and fall, I dive into my inner emptiness and find the perfect excuse to shred my skin away. When I recover, I wake up from the nightmare and start all over again. It is the snake that bites its tail. So I always insist that I need to stay strong and learn to control myself, because I don't know for how long I will be away from the trapeze."

26 years old

"Even as a child, when I was only eight or nine years old, I thought I needed a psychiatrist or psychologist, I knew I wasn't 'normal,' that I was different, in many ways, from kids around me. I also knew my family wasn't 'normal,' because the families I knew were not like mine ... And being small and feeling so alone and so weird ... It's very hard to bear. I knew that if I told an adult everything I thought and felt, first of all, they probably wouldn't take me seriously, and, secondly, they would think just that, that I'm bat crazy just because 'normal and healthy' children wouldn't bring up the things I brought up, wouldn't feel and think the things I felt and thought; so if I said it, I thought they would just see me like a strange and monstrous mutant.'

"Anyway, that feeling is often still with me nowadays ... Sometimes I think that all the people who turned away from me have done that simply because they have ended up realizing how weird and crazy I am, and perhaps it's the best they could've done for themselves, get away from someone like me... So, basically, I don't blame them for it or anything, it's almost like... I really understand them, but it makes me sad, because I would like to be different, and so perhaps these people wouldn't have had to get away from me... You told me once that you think my mother is a key part of what is happening to me... it is very possible; however, I think in relation to my worst qualities the key is my father. And don't get me wrong, I don't mean that he is to blame for how I am, not at all, but I think he has had a big influence on my almost continuous feelings of confusion, on that instability about who I am, how I really am, why sometimes I behave in such strange and changeable ways from one moment to another... And I say this because, ever since I can remember, I have lived my relationship with my father in a confusing and yet very intense way... On one hand, I felt that I hated him with all my heart, I saw him like a cruel, evil, ruthless being who did a lot of damage... On the other hand... I wanted to love him because... he was my father. And I love him, I know I love him, despite everything, and I know that, somehow, he loves me... 'Cause now that I'm no longer a little girl, I can see and understand things that a girl could not understand."

24 years old

"The situation I'm in is so complicated that it seems that nothing or no one is of any help. I have been dragging deep discomfort for many days now that has resulted in terrible pain, which obviously is not new to me, of course, but each time it comes it's like the first time, with the 'incentive' of past times. This new era is fraught with tremendous unease, great fear, and great loneliness. Loneliness that, on the other hand, is imprinted on my skin, is a part of me, was born with me, grew up with me, and is very likely to die with me. But in very few crises is it strengthened disproportionately. '

"My life revolves around a lot of uncontrolled feelings and emotions that explode inside of me. I never know when the straw that breaks the camel's back will come along, or how long I will endure. I would like to wake up one day and be someone else, I selfishly desire to be beautiful, both inside and out. Just as I am, I wish someone would be able to see this world that seems to devour people's souls through my eyes, taking everything away. I want to fill up my emptiness, fill it up with happiness, love, and beautiful things. I don't want to cry anymore because I feel lonely."

" I don't want anyone to hurt me anymore, I hurt myself more than enough. Realizing that I don't know what lies beyond this life, I would take the best of it and enjoy it. I want to leave this life feeling complete and satisfied and not escape from it with a fit of hatred towards myself."

20 years old

"Loneliness that doesn't even let go of me in the best moments or when I'm with others, it's another organ in my body that I don't even need to feed, it is self-sufficient and increases and decreases whenever it wants, it doesn't follow any rules. This 'friend' is accompanied, as I mentioned, by fear, another important organ of my humble body. This one is more frightening, this one feeds on me, invalidates me, and drains my strength; it's a terrible parasite that takes away my best virtues, nothing is ever enough and it completely destroys my defenses, fills me with angst to an unbearable point, it reproduces itself in my blood, running through my whole body and reaching my reasoning, my brain, controlling it in such a way that it reaches unsuspected places, the most remote places of my soul, where happiness resides, and it invades it completely, not letting it develop."

33 years old

"I want to keep writing because I feel like I'm drowning and I have no strength left. I was thinking about what you said and it seems unfair to me, I thought we all suffered alike in life," (Difficulty differenting self from others, their own experiences from those of others) *"but I was wrong. I haven't had hope for a while."*

"My life goes in circles, an endless nightmare, I join others and separate myself, I join again thinking I can believe and trust someone, that I have found love and I'm respected, and again I fail. I can understand I have a problem, but I can't understand why I have to suffer so much and why I fail over and over. I'm tired, I can't go on, I really don't understand, because I don't think I deserve it. I attract a lot of people, many say they love me. So, why do I make them suffer and they make me suffer? Don't I have the right to be happy? Someone tell me, because I'm going crazy!" (Problems in personal relationships, unstable and intense relationships).

"I feel on the verge of madness; I know I'm very affectionate and I give it all, but this suffering transforms me and builds up so much hatred and aggression in me that if I keep it all inside, it drowns me and gives me the feeling that I'm going crazy. I don't know how to control my anxiety, my pain, my hatred;" (Affective instability and inappropriate anger or difficulty controlling anger) *"I just know that I no longer believe in anything or anyone, I can no longer dream, I have only nightmares and fear, I constantly feel in danger and threatened. I can't forget the brutal beatings I've received and I always live with the same fear of seeing that person again... I feel threatened every day by people who are part of my life and I can't understand, if they love me so much, why they have lost respect for me or why they use me..."*

"I don't understand why I can't trust men, I couldn't even trust my other psychologist, who I trusted for many years and who let me down, they just think about having sex with me, I feel like an object. I'm frustrated, hurt, the wounds I have inside don't close, I'm burnt out, inside myself I'm a tired old lady without hope. Where am I going like this? With whom? What for? It's not worth feeling so much pain. I'm afraid of myself, very afraid, because I know one day I'll do something crazy. I will continue writing; if not, I'll do something stupid, cut myself again or kill myself..." (Recurrent suicidal behavior, gestures, or threats, or self-mutilating behavior.)

"My partner is still acting weird with me and this hurts me so much ... after our argument, he apologized, but he's still acting weird and I don't know what to do, what if he goes and leaves me?" (Efforts to avoid real or imagined abandonment.) *"I feel so helpless, and I can't stand to feel frustrated, not to receive affection, and even worse, to feel ignored, I don't know what to do, I really can't stand to be ignored, I need more, much more, and I don't have it.*

Nothing can fill this void I feel." (Chronic feelings of emptiness.) *"I want to leave and I can't, I can't do anything. I can't stand this kind of life; at least when I did drugs and worked night shifts, I felt more alive and had a good time, although this world wasn't real. Now I feel empty and unloved, alone. I want to send everything to hell and I can't... I want passion back in my life and I only had it when I did crazy stuff and lived the nightlife. In real life I just have shit, I'd rather be in hell but be able to dream. That's why I'm afraid, very afraid, because my life can't be like I want, why do I have to choose"* (dichotomous thinking) *"between being healthy, leading a healthy life and being bitter or living life, drugs, alcohol, sex, being happy and when I die, I die and that's it ..? I just can't go on like this."* (Impulsivity in at least two areas that are potentially self-damaging).

29 years old

Borderline personality disorder (BPD) is a disorder in which intense emotional instability and great internal conflict prevail. This conflict is characterized by persistent emotional chaos where the person thinks one way, feels another way, and behaves otherwise, all of them being completely different.

Due to their variability, people with this diagnosis have a difficult time defining themselves, finding out who they are, what they want, why they behave in ways that are contrary to their true desires and concerns and, above all, how to avoid this. This is a very disabling condition, difficult to understand, both for the relatives of those affected and for themselves.

These are people who often live with a sense of desperation and loneliness most of the time, thinking they have been treated unfairly (and this is often true), feeling a lack of affection, feeling that they have not been taken care of, that they are incomplete and useless, and often seeking people who can make them feel good, or in other words, who will rescue them. Some people describe it as follows:

"I need a nanny to take care of me and look after me the entire day, someone who can make this feeling of loneliness disappear so I can get on with my life."

32 years old

"I know what it is to feel alone even when you're surrounded by people. Worst of all is that I am selfish, because I have many people next to me who love me, but even that is not enough, no one is able to appease this feeling of loneliness that I have inside and I think it will be with me for the rest of my sad days."

23 years old

"I am a person who lacks perseverance, who feels inadequate, who wishes to die for not knowing how to cope with problems. I make a problem out of anything, I am unable to self-manage feelings and thoughts, which, far from being real or accurate, just complicate my life and the lives of those around me."

26 years old

"I feel there is no way out. You can't start a house from the roof, you have to start with the foundation. What can be done with a person who doesn't even have that? A person without a foundation, with nothing, a person that hates herself. A person who under the mask is not really a person. A disgusting person seeking perfection without knowing how or where and who is aware that it doesn't exist.

"When I see into other people's daily lives, I feel frightened, among all those people coming and going, I can't help but feel different and I know I'm not, but reminding me only makes me isolate myself even more and that's what I can't understand. Also, I feel like every now and then someone looks at me as if they were saying: What are you doing here? You don't fit in here! Look at yourself! You're afraid! I can smell your fear! You're pretending, but it doesn't work here, you're not real!"

25 years old

"I feel sadness, emptiness, loneliness – even when I'm with people, that I'm really not worth it at all. I'm shit. I don't love myself at all, so others will eventually realize this too and will turn away from me sooner or later. Failure and dissatisfaction with myself and my life. I have often thought and think of suicide; I think I would be better off dead, often, yes."

24 years old

"I am dependent and I always need to be with someone. Loneliness terrifies me, but it's something inside, it's a part of me and it doesn't depend any more on being accompanied or not."

32 years old

"Look at my eyes, look through them, what do you see? Do you see what I see? I can't see anything with so much pain. It squeezes me, it clings to me, it holds me like a lover and doesn't let me go. Do you see the path? Help me follow it because I don't have any strength left, I lost it in a battle against myself. Now look inside... do you see that tiny little ball??? It's me, small and helpless."

20 years old

"Sometimes I feel it's like a ping pong ball and that my feelings and thoughts control me, dominate me, throw me from side to side and I do not know how to stop it."

24 years old

"I'm sick of being a socially misunderstood person. People generally think that I don't get out of this situation because I don't try. They don't understand what this is and they associate everything with depression and think I just have to have more willpower. I do it, but it's not enough. I know that what I have is a lifestyle that needs change, it's a process of re-education in a way, but to change 32 years of an oppressive education, to change 32 years of habits or customs is not so easy. Everybody tells you things like, 'If you were with me, I would get you going,' 'If I see you like that, I'll punch you and you'll see how you'll wake up,' 'Get yourself a job and stop being locked up in the house.' The thing is, I look for a job, and another one, and another one, but I can't stand them. Is it so difficult to understand that I have a hard time starting each new day, that I would like it to always be nighttime and be in bed, that it's difficult for me to lead a normal life? And when I say normal I don't mean great big things... get up, wash up, go out... I'd want to be a baby, have someone who would hold me, cuddle me, kiss me, look after me... Someone who would do for me everything that I don't do. I don't know how to be alone, I don't like waking up and finding myself alone, I'd want to have some help starting up in the morning, someone with enough temperament and yet tactful enough to get me out of this labyrinth in which I'm stuck."

32 years old

CHANGE OF PERSPECTIVE AFTER PSYCHOEDUCATION AND THERAPEUTIC WORK

I'm not the problem, it's just a part of me

"I know what I'm about to tell you sounds like a cliché, but it's the story of my life. As long as I can remember, I have felt different from everyone else, like a freak, locked up in my own little world, not understanding my surroundings. Growing up, that feeling became more intense and caused me a great deal of suffering. I didn't fit in anywhere. I felt strange, and my greatest desire was to do anything it took to adapt. So I started turning into what people expected of me, not realizing that by doing so I was slowly losing myself. All this was topped with compulsive behaviors I did not understand, and which dominated me so that I had no control over them. I slowly fell into a depression that became chronic. I turned into a taciturn person, always sad, always looking for ways to escape from a life that felt like a prison. I tried to fly, to run away, but I couldn't. Then one of my many psychologists diagnosed me with Borderline Personality Disorder. I must say it was a relief to know that what was I was going through was not inherent to me, but a problem I was dragging since childhood. Labeling my behaviors, meeting my enemy, and finally looking at it in the eye, was what encouraged me and gave me the strength to fight it.

"Since I started therapy, I realized that I was not the problem; the problem was a small part of me, a cancer that I could remove with hard work. Much perseverance and effort is needed to fight it; I know because I've been confronting my nightmares for months now. Sometimes you're tempted to give up, but when the therapist is there encouraging you, you find strength where you thought there wasn't any. You have to learn many things. There are elements in our lives that, regardless of how much they hurt, we cannot change. We must learn to accept them and know that there are other things we can improve to enhance our quality of life.

"Sometimes negative emotions drag you down and you feel so subjugated by them that you cannot think of anything else, but there's always light at the end of the tunnel. I learned this little by little: while barely noticing, I learned many things about myself that I didn't know, I learned to love myself, to want to live, and to stop fearing the monster that distressed me so much. Again, it's not easy to cope with this, it takes hard work and perseverance, but it is worth all the suffering and fighting. You have to learn to know yourself and not depend on what others think of you. In short, you have to accept that you cannot be accepted by everyone, you don't even need this. The important thing is to be okay with yourself.

"Now, even though sometimes it's hard and I have my doubts, I know what it is to live with 'the monster' without it controlling me, to enjoy the wonderful things life offers without that nasty feeling taking over. I do not feel weird, I know that what is happening to me happens to many other people. I'm no different from others. I only have something that sometimes prevents me from doing things, but gradually its power over me is decreasing."

30 years-old

Regaining hope

"The truth is I always thought I was fine, that is, that I was an unusually healthy person. I thought the focus of my ailment was within myself, that I was unhappy because that was what I wanted, that my personality was terrible. I thought I caused myself all that suffering and it was up to me to change and stop going down hill. I never thought this was a pathology. Yes, I was depressed, I was very sensitive, I took everything to heart, I was very radical, very intolerant with myself and others, I loved and hated with devastating intensity, but 'this is how the girl is, with her big strengths and weaknesses.' Little did they know I had been quieting my daily desire to take my life for quite some time, soothing my pain, letting my mind imagine I was someone else, with a different head that did other things. Always feeling disconnected because I could not bear being inside myself, being resigned to this existence, and torturing myself for feeling miserable when I was supposed to have happiness in the palm of my hand and instead I was beating it up so I wouldn't feel it.

"I think no one can hate as much as when one hates oneself. One day, my gaze looked troubled and I guess everything inside of me started becoming more obvious to those who were next to me and loved me. They realized that I was slowly going away and sought help so I could stay.

"I had a quick diagnosis, but unlike what I thought, things did not get easier. With the limited information the psychiatrist gave us, we went to the psychologist, who was the one to help me. 'Medication alone will not be useful,' said the psychiatrist, 'you need psychotherapy or this will be complicated.' And he was right, if only the psychologist could have helped me. But he did not, at all. I could give you many examples of situations that were very unpleasant and harmful for me, but I think a couple of examples will suffice. Nowadays, I even joke about some of the things I shared with him, although at the time it wasn't funny. The pain had me numbed, and the psychologist eventually became one more person to please, like everyone else in my life, trying to guess if he had a bad day for me to have a good one, excusing his looking the other way, bored, while I spoke.

"I can now say that there was no line of work, no explanation for what was wrong with me, no answers to anything. If I'm honest, with the perspective of time, therapy consisted of criticizing my attitude to all things and offering one alternative proposal: his point of view, the only correct one. One day he called me a narcissist because I said I considered myself to be the most caring, loving, and dedicated friend. When you lack self-esteem and someone calls you narcissistic, you feel that you are even more evil and must punish yourself for it, and, Dolores, you know my punishments.

"If I asked a question about my behavior, whether it was unusual for my age to do or not do this or that (questions that arise from insecurity and fear, because today they are a part of my nature and I could care less what anyone thinks), he would tell me without hesitation that it was very rare, which made me feel even more 'special.' I think that, since he didn't understand what was happening to me, he became frustrated and, not knowing how to help me, he focused on my physical complexes, as if that were the solution to my problems. But obviously, that didn't help, because I felt so bad and so lost the last thing I could do which was to think about my looks. What also didn't help to lift my spirits is that in between sessions he repeatedly told me I was the most difficult patient in his office. One day he told me that I was not doing so bad, that he had a patient my age who still slept with a teddy bear. That day I left the office embarrassed: I was that patient, months ago I told him that detail, which he now attributed to another girl to calm me down.

"You said I could talk freely about whatever I wanted, about what had helped and what had not. What didn't help was: distrust, lack of empathy, sessions against the clock, systematic criticism, or, on the contrary, blatant flattery, attacks on my family, giving priority to what was secondary, not knowing, not having a line of work in therapy... What did help was: believing in my feelings, because if it's what I'm feeling, how can it be questioned, trusting myself, the closeness and appreciation shown, the availability at all times, the utmost respect for my family, and showing me what was happening to me, what BPD meant, and the reason for many of my behaviors. Following a treatment program that allowed me to know myself and to seek together the answers that no one seemed to have was very helpful."

27 years old

Soap bubbles are not transparent

"And here I find myself, on the edge of the world, thinking if to jump and be absorbed by it, or to continue beholding the chaos from up here, without being a part of all those things that other people don't understand."

This is the story of my life, a life that I never felt was mine until now, and now that I've owned it, takes me again outside the spiral.

I am different, different from most... when I realized it, it was too late to assume it... trying to be like them did not work for me.

I am different, I know, they all know, and I don't want to keep on trying to be like them.

Few people can experiment feelings and sensations as terrible as ours... but neither as intense nor complete, as exceptionally overwhelming, for the bad... and also for the good.

What does fog smell like? What sound do the tree trunks make when the wind blows? What does grass make you feel when you experience it with all your senses? Can you feel your own skin?, your own pores? How much of that melody fulfills you? Do you hear it vibrate and can locate those vibrations before they transform into sounds? How many reflections twinkle in the thousands of droplets that make up a wave?

To feel the Earth when you step on it with your bare feet... there are no words... to see in a mix of colors each and every hue, to identify flavors in all parts of the tongue, to distinguish each musical instrument in a song... that a smell that others can´t smell shall transport you to a faraway place and to live, in that instant, sensations in the present, to be able to experience all the feelings and sensations of a dream when you awake, and even redirect that dream in search of those sensations... Who can?

... for the good and for the bad...

The air will bring you memories... Colors will split and mix up before your eyes, sounds will be more than sound waves and you will feel them throughout your whole body, flavors will also taste of memories, people, moments...

You can learn to numb all the sensations, the good ones and bad ones, but you will always have the capacity to feel them above all.

Perhaps it might just be that we are not ready/prepared for all that information...and just that...

I see it as something that we have in addition to what other people have, something with which we are born, something that turns against us if we are not surrounded by the right people, something that can turn us into exceptional beings... or into black holes.

Perhaps it's just a matter of learning to cherish it, of not being scared of it and learning to enjoy it ...

And so... for the bad too... but also for the good...

40 years old

Part Two
Key Elements in
Borderline Personality Disorder

Chapter 5
Lack of Boundaries in People with Borderline Personality Disorder

Most people with borderline personality disorder (BPD) have great difficulty observing their own personal boundaries and those of others. There are moments when their minds, at an emotional level, are as vulnerable as the mind of a child. This is why their family members or friends sometimes describe them with phrases like, *"he is like a little kid."* This perception is partly due to the fact that they feel very fragile and vulnerable and they themselves, as well as their relatives, often realize that being exposed to the expectation that they must live as adults generates intense and disproportionate reactions to situations or details that would go unnoticed to others.

Marsha Linehan (1993a) gives a vivid description of this vulnerability. She says that people with BPD are like people with burns all over their body, who feel immense pain at the slightest touch. At times, this vulnerability makes BPD patients attach to a loved one and see this person as an extension of themselves. At such times, the chosen ones stop having rights: they become simply beings who meet their needs and they may even be bothered by the fact that they have their own lives (privacy, independence, other responsibilities). It is as if they do not know who they are, where they begin or end, and where others begin or end (alienation). Some authors believe that this is associated with emotional deprivation in the child's development.

Something else that is usually observed (especially in group sessions) is the tendency to live other people's lives. They find it much easier and interesting to get into another person's life and avoid their own. Sometimes, helping others is seen as a way to help themselves. However, and although it is easy for them to help others, the result is often quite negative, since it is a common way to avoid dealing with their own problems. Consider the example that Maria gives us:

> *"Since I've been feeling useless to society throughout my life, suddenly I find myself helping others. I can be really depressed and in my biggest crisis and then, suddenly, the alarms go off, someone needs me, is in trouble, or sick. At that moment, I stop having problems, my own are extinguished and I live for the other person, the emptiness I feel is covered because I now have something to deal with. Someone is feeling bad, really bad, I can fulfill their shortcomings, I can fill their life with love and care, I can solve their problems... a pressing need to help wakes up in me..."*

"I get to have an almost perfect life, I have something to fight for and even unconsciously, I fight for myself in my own way. It's only an apparent reality, because when that person no longer needs my help, my life collapses, the reason that placed me on top of the world ends, it vanishes."

"And now what? ... I don't know what to do with my life, the circumstances that made me wake up from my dream don't exist anymore... I feel empty again, I don't know how to fill up the time I have been occupying perhaps too intensely. Once again, I realize that my problem has not gone away, that my life is the same; my fears take over. I've only been in a fictional reality, I didn't do anything for me, I'm in the same place as before. That makes me sink again and feel even more desperate, if this is even possible... I never understand how I can care so much for another person, reaching almost 100% of my possibilities, and I'm unable to fight for myself even half of that. It is really incomprehensible. My almost perfect life was not so perfect after all, I only sustained it to meet the needs of another person."

Boundaries may or may not be observable. They are part of everyone. Knowing who we are depends largely on differentiating where we end and the other person begins. It is important to take personal responsibility and differentiate it from other people's responsibility.

An example of an observable boundary may be the space around us. This boundary can be invaded when a stranger gets too close or does so in an inappropriate way.

Lack of boundaries creates confusion and complicates the lives of people with BPD. There are different types of boundaries, but those we are interested in for this section are the physical, mental, and emotional boundaries:

1. **Physical boundaries** determine how close others can get without our feeling uncomfortable, and largely who can touch us, how, and in which situations.
2. **Mental or psychological boundaries** allow for the free expression of thoughts and opinions, but respecting those of other people.
3. **Emotional boundaries** help us manage emotions and avoid being dragged down by those of other people.

Our job as therapists is to help patients differentiate and strengthen these boundaries. Emotional boundaries are the most fragile and difficult to observe. They also greatly influence the other boundaries. People with fragile emotional boundaries will not be able to freely express their feelings, thoughts, or opinions (mental boundaries) and will have trouble differentiating physical boundaries or know when they are being invaded. This is another contradiction regarding BPD, since most people with these characteristics tend to be very observant and perceptive and this, in theory, should provide perception of boundaries in general.

Because of these contradictions, there is a tendency to focus on the negative aspects of this disorder and overlook the positive aspects that most people who suffer this illness have, such as that special sensitivity that can make their loved ones so happy during the good times. Some family members say things like: *"When she is doing well, she is the most wonderful and loving person I have ever met, but when when she is not, she behaves as if there had never been anything good between us and can even give the impression that she hates us with all her being ."* Since they feel more intensely, both the positive and the negative are magnified. Some speak of a sixth sense that allows them to know other people's moods.

As mentioned before, people with BPD tend to be more sensitive and have great empathic capacity; that is, to get in other people's shoes and understand the situations they are going through. However, sadly this does not help them relate in coherent and adaptive ways, since they have a strong tendency to focus on the negative aspects, as we will see in the following chapter.

Chapter 6
Negative Thoughts and Self-Destructive Behaviors

"It makes no sense... How can she be so hard on herself? Doesn't she realize that we all make mistakes from time to time? Can't she allow herself the slightest mistake? Can't she think that she can learn from her mistakes?"

Sometimes, the negative thoughts that people with borderline personality disorder (BPD) have about themselves are related to the information they receive. For example, if we go back to Hans Christian Andersen's tale *The Ugly Duckling*, we will remember that the duckling was considered ugly because it was different from the others. Everyone except the mother would tell him so again and again. In one version of the story, the mother was telling the following to an old duck who was criticizing the future swan:

"Look at the elegance with which he swims, and how tall he stands. Definitely, he is one of my little ones. And if you really look at him, you quickly realize that he's really cute."

However, others did not bother to notice and the duck ended up running away from everyone and isolating himself, convinced that he was horrible. He was very surprised when he finally noticed that his own reflection in the water looked just like the most beautiful animals he had ever seen: swans. Unfortunately, in many people with BPD this negative view is so ingrained that even showing them their skills is not enough. If only it were as simple as looking in a mirror.

This story is a good example of what can happen to people with BPD and can be applied to both their environment and the professionals who treat them.

As mentioned throughout this manual, sometimes working with people with BPD can be difficult, but just as the mother duck noticed the qualities of her supposedly ugly duckling, if we do the same, the possibilities of being able to reach them and being effective with therapy will be multiplied. It is very important that we trust our patients or otherwise, although unconsciously, we will transmit our mistrust. It is important to teach them the good of what they believe is bad, which is almost their whole being.

Such a negative way of thinking has a protective function for the person with BPD. It is much more difficult for them to admit their faults (frustration tolerance) if they believe they have the capacity to deal with problems and solve them. In a way, negativity allows them to better tolerate emotions, because, if they already expect to do things wrong, failure does not catch them off guard.

At times of relative stability and emotional wellbeing, they are able to reason about their negative thoughts, but when the emotion is triggered, it is as if all the mistakes from the past, each and every fault that they have committed in their life, comes back and is multiplied. The feeling of *"I messed up again, I can't do anything right, I'll never get it right"* can be so devastating for people with this problem that, when something happens that others may see as a trifle, they may react in ways that are totally disproportionate. A girl overdosed on pills because she had dropped all the books from a shelf she was organizing. She said that, at that time, she did not think there was any another solution and wanted the chaos to disappear.

This is one of the most difficult points to explain to the family, because in many cases it is related to the comments they make and the behaviors they display toward their loved ones. Sometimes, in addition to thinking that these are calls for attention, family members believe that BPD patient's behaviors are abnormal and that they are teasing; hence they transmit these thoughts in the form of judgments, gestures, behaviors, or comparisons with an assumed normality.

Although despair by the family is understandable, it is very important to understand that this extreme negativity has an adaptive function for the person with BPD. Judgments about what happened may greatly destabilize the person, who is usually aware of what happened but, at the same time, is unable to think of alternatives. Certainly, it is not of great help to receive a visit from a loved one who tells them: *"But what the hell were you thinking?! Do you think that what you did because of that nonsense was normal?!"* Perhaps a more appropriate response would be: *"I am having a hard time understanding what happened, and I won't ask you to explain it to me if you don't want to. I hope the next time something like this happens, you call me so I can help you think of other alternatives that can be less painful and harmful for you."*

In any case, these comments do not guarantee that the person will not do this behavior again. If it were that simple, they would be able to control the situation over time. However, in some cases it may work and that is why it is good to try. Perhaps it will not the first or second time around, but maybe the third or fourth time it will.

People with BPD find it hard to ask for help, their way of doing so often generates rejection by others because they cannot understand what is wanted and they end up exasperated. Others expect the person with BPD, who is in the midst of such a whirlwind of emotions and confusion, to correctly verbalize what they want and what kind of help would they like from the person to whom they are reaching out.

They need both family members and therapists to help them ask for help in a different way, and this needs to be done with practice and consistency in actions. Some family members do very well for a while, but the moment the person improves, they usually relax and take this improvement for granted, thus neglecting their way of responding to certain situations, and confusing and invalidating the person.

What is this invalidation? Roughly and as an example, it happens when the needs of a person are not respected and their feelings, thoughts, or behaviors are denied or questioned. In order to simplify this, I will explain it in terms of family and children. Many thoughts, behaviors, and feelings that people with BPD have may seem inadequate or maladaptive. In order to understand the effect of invalidation, it may be easier to imagine them for a moment as vulnerable children who need support, understanding, and someone to tell them what is and is not right in a loving and calm way, without judgment. However, we must not forget that they are adults and want to and should be treated as adults. It is also important to take into consideration that this invalidating form of communication is common among adults, couples, friends, etc.

The invalidating family is one that does not respect the needs of the children, denying their emotions, thoughts, behaviors, and feelings, and even attributing their own to them. Of course, there are different forms of invalidation and, often, this invalidation is entirely unconscious. For example, imagine that a child comes home and has something important to tell his mother. In turn, she is concerned about a problem she had with a neighbor and about finishing dinner on time. The child starts telling his mother what happened and she pretends to listen, but continues thinking about her own problems as she moves around the kitchen without making eye contact with her child. The child realizes that his mother is not paying attention and leaves feeling ignored. The mother does not even realize what just happened, she just keeps doing her chores.

Can this situation inadvertently get even worse?

Of course it can, let us imagine that the same day the child is still hurt and angry and refuses to try the food, the mother gets angry and asks, *"What is the matter with you?"* The boy replies, *"I was telling you before, but you didn't listen to me"* and the mother, feeling angry, says, *"As if I didn't have more important things to do than listen to your nonsense."* Although it is a simple comment that we can say in a moment of anger, it is an example of invalidation, because the child is being told that his problems and feelings are nonsense.

To explain this to parents and patients, an example of a classical Spanish joke may be appropriate:

> "What is a sweater? Something that the child wears when the mother is cold."

Although this may be simply an attempt at mind reading by mothers, the consequence may be that the child feels invalidated if he does not want to put on the sweater because he is hot. This scenario will be very familiar to parents and children.

Have we ever seen or witnessed a situation where a child says he is hungry and the parent replies, *"You're not hungry, you just ate,"* or the child says he is hot and he is told, *"Don't be silly, how can you be hot when it's freezing cold?"* Obviously, these comments may not affect some children at all, especially when they occur sporadically, but when they are common and long-term, they do become a problem, since the child and future adult learns to doubt his own emotions.

UNDERSTANDING DESTRUCTIVE BEHAVIORS IN PEOPLE WITH BORDERLINE PERSONALITY DISORDER

Some people with BPD are willing to endure anything in order to feel loved and accepted. Their need for acceptance may even make them endure physical or psychological abuse by other people, for fear of being abandoned, judged, or criticized. It is as if having your own opinion were not a good thing. Many feel that since they are like this, they do not have the right to have opinions and, if they do, they are always wrong.

It is important to understand that, in many cases, for the person with BPD, these destructive, manipulative, or maladaptive behaviors actually have an adaptive function. They act that way because it is what they have learned, what they have been doing for years, and in most cases, they receive responses that reinforce this behavior. For example, many people with BPD, instead of talking about their feelings, act them out. This is because they learn that action results in a response of attention, concern, or closeness from others, while talking about feelings often brings up negative responses such as anger, rejection, or invalidation.

Self-destructive behaviors by some people with BPD, such as cutting, burning, banging their heads against the wall, scratching, stabbing, and slapping themselves, often generate great confusion among relatives and friends. They struggle to understand and assimilate these behaviors. A relative may comment: *"How is it possible that cutting brings her relief? It just makes no sense! How can she ask me to accept that behavior?"*

Even if it is difficult to understand, the truth is that many people with BPD feel relief when they make cuts in their skin. It is as if they hurt themselves to escape from their body or to deal with emotions that are too intense and overwhelming. When emotions increase in intensity and can no longer be contained, they need to find a way out. Although it may sound ironic, people with BPD sometimes resort to self-destructive behavior as a comforting strategy for the discomfort they feel.

Some people say that they need to have control over their pain. It is as if they need to have a real reason to feel bad.

> *"I need to feel pain for something real. You don't know what it's like to feel this bad without an apparent reason, it makes me feel selfish, like a bad person. There are people in the world who have real reasons to feel bad and here I am feeling sorry for myself, with everything I have."*

There may be a variety of reasons for self-destructive behavior: fear, anxiety, a sense of failure (punishment for failing), anger towards others, self-punishment, despair, etc. Sometimes it is a way to ask for help or communicate how bad they feel. Other times it is a form of self-punishment that comes from feelings of guilt such as, *"I deserve it,"* *"I'm not valid,"* *"I'm a bad person,"* and other times, as described before, to feel alive or feel pain for something real.

One patient, who usually goes to dangerous places and befriends difficult people, explained the following while sobbing and crying:

> *"When I start a fight, I'm hoping that someone will stab me or shoot me, because that would put an end to this hell and I wouldn't have to suffer anymore. I don't have the balls to kill myself."*

Paradoxically, self-mutilation and compulsive, abusive, or self-destructive behaviors often lead to a temporary feeling of calm and even euphoria, even if they later have the opposite effect and generate feelings of discomfort and guilt, in other words, feeling even worse than before the destructive act.

Self-harm or compensatory behaviors, such as resorting to substance abuse, reckless driving, binge eating or not eating, sex, etc., often have a regulatory function for the person with BPD, so we are interested in seeing beyond the symptom. In any case, it is important to help them understand their own self-destructive behaviors in order to work on them and, eventually, replace them with others that are less harmful.

It is important to remember that people with this disorder often come to therapy because they feel bad and they may not be able to specify what is happening to them or what is interfering with their quality of life. Often, they can neither name their emotions nor find a relationship between their problems and the things that have happened. They may not know which situations make them feel worse or if these problems occur in the presence of certain people. They often come in with many doubts, feeling lost and looking for answers that may alleviate the uncertainty that is generally present in their lives. Understanding the motives behind the symptoms is the best way to organize an adequate treatment plan.

Chapter 7
Lack of Identity in People with Borderline Personality Disorder

"Depending on my mood, I change colors. If I feel threatened, the change is much more intense, faster, and disconcerting for those around me. My eyes move independently in many directions: there is no apparent coordination. My tongue catches the food I want to eat. Just at that moment, I seem to acquire life and movement."

This chameleon metaphor reflects many aspects of people with borderline personality disorder (BPD). In addition to revealing their desperate attempts to adapt to the environment and to other people, it shows how others perceive them, as well as the confusion generated by their changes. Changes in the chameleon's color manifest the character changes that take place depending on the person's moods, which are magnified if they feel threatened. Depending on the requirements of the situation, they change colors. This is not intentional manipulation, but an attempt to fit into the environment. It is a defense mechanism that allows them to deal with different situations. However their chameleon changes do not always produce the result they want, because they often choose the wrong color.

A chameleon's eyes move independently in many directions. Emotions, thoughts, and behaviors of individuals with BPD function similarly: each one is different and independent; instead, they should work in a coordinated fashion. That is, they think, feel, and behave in completely different ways and these are generally the opposite of what they want to convey. The greater the lack of integration, the greater the difficulties they have functioning in a coordinated manner.

The tongue exemplifies how they can hold on to what they want to achieve. Although in the case of the chameleon it is usually related to food, people with BPD sometimes feed off other people and desperately cling to them. Just as the chameleon seems to suddenly come alive when food appears, people with BPD act impulsively when their buttons are pushed, without thinking for a second about the consequences of their behavior – especially when they want to get something or someone's attention. This occurs because when people are feeling so much pain and have so little hope, they need to hold on to other people's energy to keep on going. They have so little self-confidence that other people's proposals are overvalued and seen as possible solutions to their problems. We can also use the metaphor of the chameleon to illustrate the behavior of people with BPD, because the rest of the time it moves in slow motion, as if waiting for a new signal from the outside world to react.

Similarly, people with BPD cling to whatever or whoever brings them immediate possible solutions. The rest of the time, they often feel hopeless, apathetic, and empty, waiting for a person or situation that might ease their pain, fill their void, or make them react.

BPD is obviously much more complex than this, but if we consider that many of these behaviors are associated with an attempt to adapt and a struggle to move on, we will be able to understand many of the issues that need to be addressed and explained to people with this diagnosis during therapy. If we just see them as manipulative and problematic people, we will hardly be able to help them understand what is happening to them and, above all, how to cope in more positive ways.

> *"I find it easier to adapt to what is expected of me and to other people's way of being (their opinions, standards, tastes, etc.). I find it hard to show myself as I am, because the few times I've done it, the results were horrible. They've hurt me a lot and I've felt naked and betrayed. I don't have the courage to look these people in the eye. I feel small, insignificant, and stupid for thinking that someone could really love me as I am."*

Many people with BPD have great difficulty trusting themselves. Lack of confidence, low self-esteem, and feeling ill-prepared to have an opinion, decide, or be right, often leads them to base their decisions on the opinions of others. Since they do not have a defined identity, they search for one and usually protect themselves or impress others by taking on different roles, depending on the moment or the people they meet. In many cases, what they are trying to avoid is being known (for fear of rejection or abandonment) or having other people find out their weaknesses, so that they will not get hurt. Often, instead of looking for solutions and focusing on the things that can work or that have worked before, they look to other people or things in order to satisfy their needs. They cling to anything or anyone they may think is willing and able to provide this.

Some people with BPD, especially those who feel empty, believe they are not able to avoid this persistent shifting. It is as if their power of decision and personal choice disappears. In times of need, they need to cling desperately to whatever is closest in their environment. This can range from substance abuse, sexual encounters with one or more people they just met, going away with a group of strangers for a few days, bingeing on food, etc.

Our job as professionals is to help patients realize that, actually, nothing and no one can give them what they are searching for and that such a way of acting is particularly dangerous. After each moment of disillusion comes disappointment and the person may break down for a while or express anger or pain in different ways, thus increasing discomfort and confusion. In these cases, one of the problems that may complicate the prognosis is substance addiction. It is important to differentiate that, in the case of people with BPD, substance abuse and behavioral compulsions are probably related to difficulty tolerating and regulating emotions. In times of anxiety, confusion, or frustration, those with BPD get carried away by the first thing that comes their way or goes through their head. It is something they learned in order to ease their discomfort. But, like everything that is learned, it can be unlearned.

Many people with BPD are used to living in the extremes. Through therapy, it is possible to teach them that there are alternatives and that they do not have to live in chaos, they can attack and resolve it. In order for this to be possible, it is important to help them see that it will not be achieved using compensatory behaviors and that if they do these, they will usually end up with more problems than they already have (substance dependence, eating disorders, sexual diseases, etc.).

To address these issues, it is very important to understand that many people with BPD feed on intensity to survive. For some, it is a way of feeling that they are alive and some may even come to believe that they could not bear to live without intense experiences.

> *"What am I like? The truth is I don't know. I'm not sure what I want, or what I like, or what I can do. One day I wake up thinking that I know who I am or that I know what I want, but I soon realize that I'm following something I've seen or heard. For example, one day I watch a movie and find myself fantasizing about the story, thinking I could lead the life of the main character. Another day, I listen to someone I find interesting and then I realize I'm imitating her (her mannerisms, her way of talking, her tastes...). In the end, I'm never myself, but I just don't know how to be me. What is that? Who am I? What do I really like? What am I going to do with my life? I don't have the slightest idea. That's what I would like to know. Can you give me an answer?"*

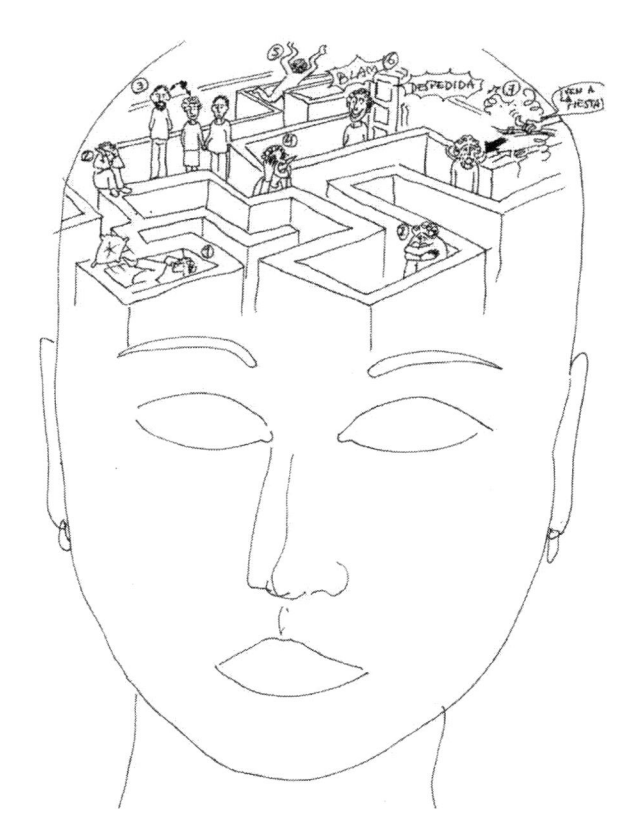

One of the main therapeutic goals is the integration of the personality, which is usually achieved gradually. To understand the role of identify disturbance in BPD, we can compare it to a disorganized, mixed up, and incomplete puzzle. This image speaks to the importance of laying a foundation that will allow the person to get enough peace and balance to establish those aspects with which they identify and differentiate them from those that are related to learning or lack of resources.

In the psychoeducational program *Rough Diamonds II* (Mosquera, 2004b. 2013b), one module focuses on identity disturbance. The ultimate goal is to help patients discover their true identity, which is usually hidden behind symptoms and behaviors that keep them in an unstable and chaotic situation. This process can be explained by using a puzzle metaphor.

1. **Complete but disorganized pieces:** When we start psychotherapy, we often observe that some people with BPD feel lost, confused, and have difficulty with boundaries and perception of self and their surroundings. Often, they do not know how to show themselves or act.

2. **Incomplete pieces:** In some cases, we observe that, while trying to put puzzle together, it becomes clear that there are missing pieces and, in addition to placing those that already exist, we must create new ones, i.e., providing the person with skills and resources.

3. **Mixed up pieces**: In some cases, some pieces are already assembled, some are disorganized, and others have been taken from other puzzles. In these cases, our work will be directed toward helping the patient identify the real pieces, differentiating them from those that have been learned or imposed, and finally organizing them. Many patients, in an effort to fit in, look for signals in others and assume that these are their own, in a desperate attempt to fit in. For some patients, the BPD diagnosis ends up becoming an identity hallmark (Mosquera, 2004a, 2010), which they hold on to largely due to the absence of a strong self-concept and the difficulties they encounter in truly getting in touch with their emotions and needs. Often, they have not established differentiation between themselves (self) and the external world, which leads them to have a significant feeling of confusion. In these cases, it is important that while assembling the puzzle, we put each piece in its place and carefully remove the pieces that belong in other puzzles (learning). In cases with many borrowed pieces, it is important to carefully disassemble these borrowed puzzle pieces, because otherwise the real pieces can break during the process.

When we take this into account and work carefully on the issues that interfere with identity (emotional instability, lack of boundaries, need to fill the void or fit in, lack of adaptive resources to manage their relationships and their discomfort, unresolved trauma, etc.), there is usually a decrease in the feeling of chaos, uncertainty, and dependency on others (including the belief in needing them to survive) and an increased sense of autonomy and control of their own lives. This organizing work helps people with BPD build and develop their own identity, eliminating the effects of maladaptive learning and environments that may have interfered with their development. The process is similar to the careful assembly of a puzzle in which the end result will be the discovery of the person and the integration of the personality.

LACK OF IDENTITY: A PATIENT'S ARTISTIC EXAMPLE

This 26-year-old woman's drawing is a good example of the lack of identity (both figures lack faces). It actually exemplifies much more than this. The little girl on the left represents her most vulnerable part that needs safety and security. The geisha exemplifies her destructive part and her guilt. The geisha is the part who gives herself away and acts according to what others expect of her, regardless of her own feelings or desires. She is the one who has no opinions of her own and thinks she has no right to have them. The flames exemplify the anger she feels about all this (toward herself and others). The eye above is her fear of criticism, the feeling of being watched and judged by everyone, at all times.

When identity disturbance represents a deep fragmentation of the self, it may indicate severe dissociative symptoms that may not be apparent unless specifically explored. In some patients, we can see what Fonagy (2000) and other authors call *"strange experience"* within the self: thoughts or feelings that are experienced as part of the self, but do not seem to belong in it. According to Dell and O'Neill (2009), these intrusive phenomena are the core element of dissociative symptomatology, as we will see in the following chapter.

Chapter 8
Dissociation and Borderline Personality Disorder

"A well-integrated personality has a first person perspective of the self, the others and the environment, an integrative capacity and adaptive behaviors in the world. It includes the capacity to self-regulate and reflect."

Van der Hart, Nijenhuis, & Steele (2006)

Identity is characteristically distorted in borderline personality disorder (BPD); it is unstable, poorly developed and variable. In the more extreme cases, the question *"Who am I really?"* becomes impossible to answer. People with BPD can change radically from one moment to the next to the point of not remembering anything they have done or said. They do or say things, but do not recognize themselves in them: *"It's as if it wasn't me."* Sometimes there are thoughts in their heads that are very different from their usual thinking, which at times take the form of voices. They suffer from internal battles, which at times completely block and consume the individual. During these battles, people may feel as if they had different parts inside themselves, aspects that are so radically different and separate that they function on their own, without the individual being able to control what they do or what they say. On the contrary, sometimes these parts of the personality are the ones controlling the person's thoughts, feelings, or actions.

Citing the *Diagnostic and Statistical Manual of Mental Disorders*, fifth edition (DSM-5, 2013), dissociative disorders are characterized by "an impairment in the integrative functions of consciousness, identity, memory, and perception of the environment." Consciousness is impaired to different degrees in BPD. In many cases, individuals are not fully aware of what they do or what they generate, and the apparent lucidity they sometimes show contrasts with other times of extreme agitation or behavioral alterations that, to some extent, could be understood as altered states of consciousness. Identity, the definition of who I am, may be blurry in some cases, but in others it is characterized by ambivalence, instability, and rejection of certain aspects of themselves, very similar to what we see in those with dissociative disorders. Amnesia for certain life periods or specific moments in time is common in many borderline patients.

Their perception of the environment, the world they see, can be radically different depending on their mental state, as we see so very clearly in the descriptions they make of their partners when at the extremes of idealization and devaluation.

Dissociative disorders appear as a consequence of severe, early, or long-term traumatic experiences. Since many BPD patients present with severe trauma histories, in clinical presentations of greater severity it is understandable that both phenomena coincide. But even in cases of BPD with mild or moderate functional impairment, we can see many shared aspects with more overtly dissociative clinical pictures.

Another element that is considered essential in developing a dissociative disorder is the presence of early, disorganized attachment. An example would be when the primary caregiver is a person suffering from numerous symptoms of severe traumatic experiences. When the child gets angry, the mother may become blocked because memories of abuse by her father become activated in her own nervous system. Or, when the child cries, a mother suffering from a severe depression may feel powerless to contain or regulate her child's emotion, since she is unable to regulate her own emotional state. Another example would be when there is mistreatment or clear abuse within the family, for example, an alcoholic parent who is directly violent with the child or the other parent. Fear of lack of recognition and acceptance characterizes the child's bond with primary caregivers. Without the mirror of a caregiver who accepts them as they are, children may not develop an integrative view of themselves as complete beings. Aspects of the child's emotional needs not accepted by the attachment figures may be rejected, not recognized, or externalized by the child and the future adult. In extreme cases, a part of the personality will be dissociated, split, concealed, or rejected, which will affect the functioning of the mind in different ways (Mosquera & González, 2011).

When these disorganizing situations take place, people's minds lack the ability to integrate all that they have lived and everything they are. There are experiences that the brain has not been able to assimilate and which remain in their consciousness as if time had not passed. When those memories become activated, people feel as though they are "back there and then". If it is a childhood memory, they can literally feel like a child or behave as a child. If it is a negative situation with an ex-boyfriend, for example, the person may react to the current partner *as if* she were facing the former partner. And as commented before, in cases where dissociation is more pronounced, it can reach a point during those episodes where the person does not remember what happened and even functions as a completely different person.

In borderline personality disorder, regardless of the degree of dissociation, there is difficulty integrating everything the person is. Certain personal traits, certain reactions, will generate rejection or distress in the individual. When there is an extreme phobic attitude towards some aspects of the self, these can be externalized and experienced as foreign. For example, people may reject their anger; sometimes due to having experienced the consequences of other people's uncontrolled rage, other times because they were never allowed to express anger or disagreement.

That which we cannot accept, we are unable to handle. When it comes up, negative emotional reactions are triggered, we stop thinking reflectively, and all we can do is try to control it. But control is always a temporary maneuver, which does not fit every scenario and does not always work. Sometimes, there are things we cannot control; sometimes our self-control is overwhelmed. Then, the reaction we try to contain becomes triggered and we have no tools to regulate or manage it. If this reaction is, for example, anger, it will come up as pure rage, blind rage, or uncontrolled rage. Individuals will not feel in control, will not feel like themselves, and later may not remember, in full or in part, what happened in those cases with a higher level of dissociation. This anger may manifest only internally as contained rage, which, when dissociated, takes the form of thoughts that come up suddenly for the person or critical or insulting voices.

Dissociation of the personality and lack of integration would explain many of the seemingly incomprehensible changes seen in people with BPD. They do not usually have elaborated parts with a first-person perspective. Instead, they tend to speak of different aspects of themselves: *"The bad Marta, the good Marta, the happy Marta, the sad Marta."* When individuals with BPD have severe dissociation, different parts of the personality may be elaborated, which they may call by different names, with whom they may interact, and who may take control or present thoughts, memories, feelings, or behaviors that the person feels as alien, strange, or surprising (for more information, see Mosquera, Gonzalez, & Van der Hart, 2011).

Let us see some artistic examples of the internal system of patients:

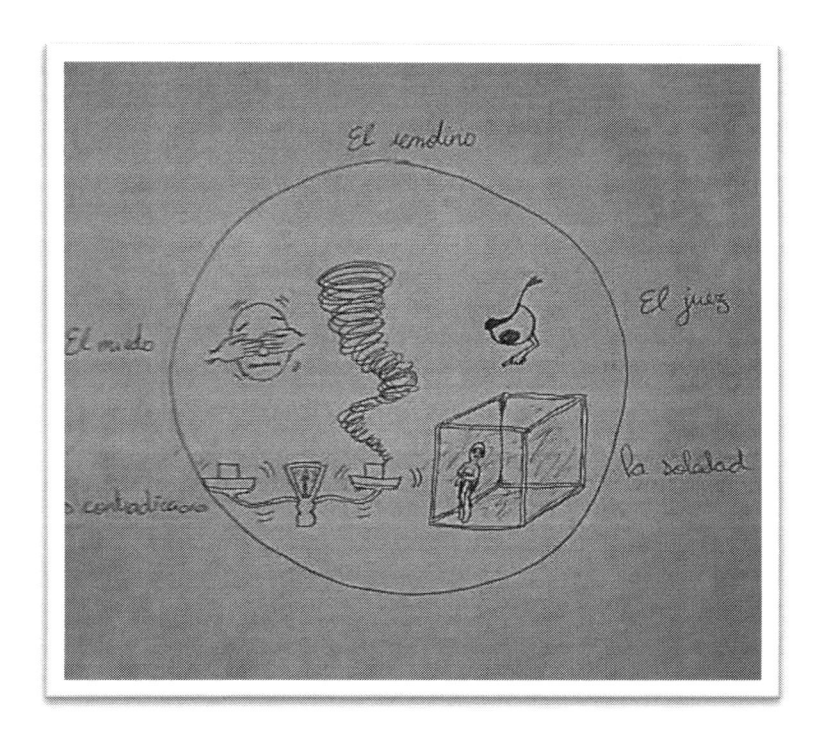

Fig. 1 & 2: *Drawings of the internal system of a patient with BPD and Other Specified Dissociative Disorder in different stages of treatment*

These symptoms may be there without being obvious to those around them. For example, voices or auditory hallucinations may occur for years, but people are used to living with them. They are afraid of not being understood or being seen as crazy if they talk about it. So they do not talk about it or they hide it, even when asked specifically. Other times, family members perceive these radical changes in behavior more clearly and realize that sometimes patients are not themselves, that they are in an altered state of consciousness.

In addition to the fragmentation of identity and consciousness, and memory problems, another frequent dissociative symptom is emotional disconnection. People can sometimes feel disconnected from their emotions, and go through very extreme moments of connection, without a middle ground or the ability to think about their emotions. Sometimes, people with BPD self-injure to cause themselves physical pain and, thus, get away from the even more intolerable emotional pain (Mosquera, 2008). At other times, when dissociation is greater, they may self-injure without feeling the pain; somehow, they are able to self-anesthetize. Sometimes, they function on automatic pilot without real awareness of what they are doing, or they may literally see themselves from outside their body. Their image in the mirror may seem strange to them, or even unfamiliar. At times, what surrounds them is what feels strange, as if it were a dream or a movie. These depersonalization and derealization symptoms co-occur in many mental disorders and may appear as isolated symptoms in patients with BPD, although their level of dissociation may not be very intense.

WHY IS DISSOCIATION IMPORTANT IN BORDERLINE PERSONALITY DISORDER?

Dissociative disorders are one of the most common comorbid diagnoses in BPD, and their presence implies greater complexity and some particular characteristics at the time of treatment. If patients cannot remember important moments of their life, or if when connecting to certain experiences they go right into the past, therapists must be careful in the initial examination, so individuals do not become overwhelmed and can gradually understand what is happening once their confidence starts increasing.

The higher the dissociation, the more carefully we will have to go into aspects of which the patient is not yet aware or about which the patient cannot bear to think. It is equally important that therapists, understanding this difficulty, adjust the pace of the work, yet without fearing exploration of these aspects masked by dissociation. Understanding the origins of their problems is helpful for patients who have lived through more complex and traumatic experiences. We must simply find a balance between respecting defenses and exploring.

Exploring dissociative symptoms is not only important for the therapist and for the diagnosis. It is very helpful for patients to be able to discuss these symptoms, which they frequently have never been able to discuss with anyone and are an important part of their inner experience. Making them fill out a simple dissociation scale allows an initial assessment, from which to delve deeper into this part of the problem. A very simple and useful screening tool is the Dissociative Experiences Scale (DES) (Bernstein & Putnam, 1986), provided that we do not just pay attention to the numerical scores. Instead we must explore how these issues take place in their lives by asking for examples from the patient's experience for each of the positive items.

Fifty-nine percent of BPD patients met DSM-IV criteria for one of the dissociative disorders compared to 22% of patients without BPD (Ross, 2007). Numerous studies support that dissociative disorders, especially dissociative identity disorder, are the result of severe and repeated psychological trauma, which usually begins in childhood (Braun, 1990; Chu, 1991; Bernstein & Putnam, 1986; Coons & Milstein, 1986; Ross, 2007; Saxe et al., 1993; Van der Kolk & Kadish, 1987).

CAN WE BETTER UNDERSTAND SOME OF BPD SYMPTOMS IF WE TAKE DISSOCIATION INTO CONSIDERATION?

Some people with BPD tend to hyperactivate, reacting from a state that began to develop in childhood; in the present, this response seems maladaptive and apparently disproportionate. Other people, instead of becoming activated, will tend to disconnect, and, in severe cases, to the point of not remembering what happened during this disconnection.

These dissociative defense mechanisms that were learned, and which were useful and adaptive in early periods of trauma, are now maladaptive and disconcerting. Therefore, they are not only ineffective, but generate more problems.

Case example

A patient calls the emergency services. She is crying, very upset, and has difficulty breathing. She explains the terrible things her boyfriend has said and done. An appointment is set. When the patient comes to the office, she comes in hand in hand with her partner and seems calm, as if nothing had happened. The therapist asks if they -she and her partner- have solved their problems. At first the patient seems confused and asks, "*What do you mean?*" When the therapist asks about what had happened, the patient becomes emotionally active, screams, and cries due to the pain he had inflicted on her. In this case, the patient had dissociated the information of what had happened the day before, because the intensity of the discomfort from the situation experienced was intolerable for her.

When dissociation is less pronounced, we can observe the same phenomenon -sudden changes in emotional state- without amnesia.

Patients with BPD often have dramatically different perspectives of the world around them, of the people they relate to, or of themselves. When we talk with patients about these issues in a calm state, what they say or seem to understand or recognize in that state is not automatically transferable or applicable to other states. Sometimes, the patient comes into the office, or relates to other people in some environments, from what the theory of structural dissociation of the personality (Van der Hart, Nijenhuis, & Steele, 2006) calls the *apparently normal part of the personality*. At times of emotional activation, they may function from a defensive and reactive *emotional part of the personality*. For example, when acting from the *apparently normal part of the personality*, people may ask for help (but then reject it when an emotional part of the personality who learned not to trust gets triggered).

A common example is one where the patient may feel terribly sorry for having used drugs and beats himself up non-stop for the damage this does, both to himself and to those around him. However, sometimes, even fostered by the anguish and lack of energy in which his critical thoughts and constant beating up submerge him, he tries to resolve his distress by consuming once again. As he heads off to find another dose, none of the statements of guilt, none of the negative consequences this may have, come to mind. At that point, his only objective is to achieve a feeling he does not see how to obtain otherwise. It is as if the territories of guilt and that of irresponsible pursuit of instant gratification never come in contact. The information on the problems of consuming is not accessible in the state of searching for more intoxication. With an integrative and reflective ability, they would be able to say "*on the one hand I would like to take this, but on the other hand I see that it could bring many problems, so I choose not to use.*" In the absence of this integrative and reflective ability the patient simply goes from responsibility in the form of guilt to absolute irresponsibility, unable to find a middle ground or a balance point (Mosquera & González, 2012).

These changes of mind can lead to frustration, confusion, and even hostility in the patient's relatives or their therapists, who may interpret them simply as lack of motivation or deliberate lies. If instead we understand the world of non-integrative contradictory extremes described by dissociation, we can gain a global perspective of these individuals' problem that leads to new therapeutic opportunities.

DISSOCIATIVE SYMPTOMS IN BORDERLINE PERSONALITY DISORDER

Depersonalization

Many people with BPD talk about feeling like observers of themselves. Although this feeling is common in many other diagnoses, it may be particularly disconcerting for those who lack an identity and have persistent fears and insecurities. Despite the confusion it causes, it is just a defense mechanism, a way of coping with discomfort at certain times. Some people, for example, when they fear losing control, take distance from themselves. In these cases, we can speak of mild, temporary, or transient depersonalization and not consider it a separate disorder.

Let us see some frequent examples:

- I have acted automatically while the real me was far from what was happening to me.
- I have felt I was living in a dream.
- I've seen myself from afar, as if I was outside of my body, watching a movie of myself.
- I feel I can disconnect or separate myself from my emotions.
- My behavior has escaped my control.
- I have hurt myself on purpose in order to feel pain or feel that I am real.
- I have had the feeling of being a stranger to myself or I have not recognized myself in the mirror.
- A part of me does things, while another part of me who is observing talks to me about them.
- I have felt like parts of my body were disconnected from the rest of the body.
- My whole body or parts of it have seemed strange or unreal.
- I have felt as if words came out of my mouth without being under my control.

Derealization

The feeling of strangeness, of not knowing what is real or not, or of living in a dream is something that many people with BPD describe.

> "Every day is worse than the previous one; I feel tired, everything takes a huge effort and I would like to know how to deal with it better, but I have a hard time living in the present. At times, I feel that I am not part of this web, of this set, as if I were able to see it from the outside, as if they didn't see me. This leads me to an objective understanding of the world. If I don't have interests, motivations... I am more objective because I'm less selfish than the rest, but I also realize that this is a fantasy."

Here are some examples:

- Some people or places that I know have seemed unfamiliar.
- I sometimes feel like I was looking at the world with fogged up glasses or through a fog and people or things seem unclear or distant.
- Some friends, family, or my environment have seemed strange or unreal.
- I have felt like the people around me belonged only in a dream.
- It seemed like someone was becoming another person.
- Although I am aware of who my parents are, I have felt as if they were really not related to me.
- I have had trouble recognizing friends, family, or my home.
- I have gotten confused about what was real or unreal around me.
- I have had the impression that some people or places I know have faded or disappeared.

Derealization and depersonalization usually manifest when there is a disconnection between the self and the environment.

Identity Disturbance

- I have mood swings that I can't control.
- I have temper tantrums that seem to escape my control or are disproportionate to the situation.
- I have different names that I give myself or that other people call me.
- I don't recognize things written by me.
- I feel like I'm living a secret life and not even my best friends know who I really am.
- I sometimes speak in a totally different way and with another voice.
- I feel like I have a public persona and a private one.
- People tell me that I have acted like a different person.
- I'm an adult and I have imaginary friends with whom I speak.
- I feel as if the child inside of me took control of my behavior.
- I feel as if I had several people inside that influence my behavior and my mood.

Amnesia

Amnesia is usually mentioned by people who have forgotten all or part of an episode or life stage. It can range from hours to sometimes years, or for a particular event that had a high emotional intensity. For many, this is equivalent to being distracted or having bad memory, but when we explore further, we observe that this amnesia only happens at times when the patient has experienced a traumatic event or during a period of greater discomfort (e.g., a severe disease of a close relative).

Amnesia can be of different types:

- **Amnesia of the past**: *"I don't remember what happened between five and ten years old," "The memories of my childhood are hidden inside of me," "My life is a puzzle with missing pieces," "I don't remember anything about my childhood (*after *five years of age)."*
- **Conscious recent amnesia**: memory lapses, difficulty remembering daily activities, or forgetting important personal information such as name, age, address, or date of birth. Sometimes, they are moments of the day: *"Sometimes, there are hours of the day of which I have no memories."*
- **Unconscious amnesia**: *"I have found myself in unexpected places and I couldn't remember how I got there," "I find objects in my house that belong to me, but I can't remember how or when I acquired them, or writings I don't remember doing," "I see myself doing something and don't remember when or how I started doing it," "Others talk to me about things I don't remember."*

Other symptoms such as flashbacks, conversion symptoms, and pseudo-psychotic symptoms, such as auditory or visual hallucinations, may also be explained from the point of view of dissociation. Often, people who suffer from such symptoms have a hard time describing them and fear that these experiences or feelings may mean that they are crazy.

The concepts of fragmentation and dissociation may help us understand many of the seemingly disproportionate symptoms and behaviors in borderline pathology. Although experiences related to dissociative symptoms are quite common, it is important to note that not all of them necessarily occur in all patients with BPD.

Part Three
Assessment

Chapter 9
Diagnosing Borderline Personality Disorder

Assessment and diagnosis of borderline personality disorder (BPD) and other personality disorders is a complex task, as it must take into account many aspects of the individual's life and not simply limit itself to presenting complaints or problems.

Although there are numerous diagnostic tools, the clinical interview is undoubtedly the best way to assess the presence of BPD. Professionals conducting the interview must have in-depth knowledge not only of the various diagnostic criteria in the manuals, but also of how to treat each of these and what type of questions to ask in order to assess their presence and relevance. We must also have the resources and skills needed to address a variety of aspects, since patients are not always aware of their problems and often are not inclined to talk about them in detail. This is especially true in cases of complex trauma, where confronting painful memories can destabilize them or make them feel guilty. When doing so, they run the risk of becoming emotionally naked. It is important to have answers to help them feel understood, as this will encourage them to cooperate during the interview and consider the possibility of starting therapy.

In this regard, it should be noted that the standardized assessment tools (tests) and/or structured or semi-structured interviews may be helpful in exploring some aspects not explicitly addressed during the diagnostic interview and they can provide additional information, but they must not be used as the sole or primary source of evaluation. The intention is not to downplay questionnaires, scales, or the various tests that exist for evaluating this disorder, but to highlight the importance of psychological interviews, interactional aspects, and therapeutic observation as crucial diagnostic tools.

Although according to the DSM-5, the presence of five or more BPD diagnostic criteria may indicate the existence of this disorder, it is important to take into consideration that, to some extent, we **all** have some of these traits, especially adolescents. In order to consider a possible diagnosis, these characteristics should be of long-duration (years), persistent, and intense.

In addition, we must keep in mind that many of these standardized instruments can lead to false diagnoses (both positive and negative):

- **False diagnoses (positive):** it is possible to diagnose a disorder that does not exist. This is because many of the elements contained in the **diagnostic criteria** (*Diagnostic and Statistical Manual of Mental Disorders* [DSM] and *International Classification of Diseases* [ICD]) refer to personality traits that, at low intensity levels, are present in many people with no apparent problems. Due to the tendency of BPD patients to have doubts about their way of being and feel identified with the things they see in others, they may answer yes to some aspects they perceive in other people and would like to have as part of their personal repertoire (imitation).
- **False diagnoses (negative):** this is possible because the lack of awareness of the illness in some people with BPD can make them respond negatively to indicators of pathology with which they do not identify or still cannot accept in themselves (consciously or unconsciously).

Therefore, it is especially important to pay attention to the psychological interview and to remind family members, as well as people who may possibly be affected and who think they may have the disorder based on something they have read, that a diagnosis should not be based on the contents of a prospectus, a website, or a book, and that they must be careful when diagnosing themselves or other people.

It is important to highlight that in diagnosing BPD, we need to be especially cautious, pay attention to what is not immediately apparent, and not get carried away by first impressions. There is still a predisposition to diagnose and thus treat the symptom, that is, what is apparent and obvious at the time of therapy, such as eating disorders, depressive symptoms, etc. International diagnostic classifications are designed to reflect the most visible problems and focus on symptoms. Since BPD is often associated with adverse early experiences (Zanarini, Yong, Frankenburg, et al., 2002; Mosquera, Gonzalez, & Van der Hart, 2011; Mosquera & González, 2011), trauma-oriented psychotherapeutic approaches, attachment problems, and parenting styles can help us better understand where and how the patient's difficulties and symptoms began. Therapies such as EMDR Therapy (Shapiro, 1989), Cognitive-Analytic Therapy (Ryle & Kerr, 2002), Mentalization-based Therapy (Bateman & Fonagy, 2004), Transference Focused Psychodynamic Therapy (Clarkin, Yeomans, & Kernberg, 1998), and Schema Therapy (Young, 1994) allow us to understand the contribution of life experiences in the development of BPD and thus suggest a more integrative approach to the disorder.

People with BPD often come to therapy feeling burned out, apathetic, lacking in confidence and, therefore, may adopt a defensive attitude: *"We'll see if this guy is going to tell me something I don't already know," "What will she think if I tell her what is really happening to me? She'll certainly think I'll have to be admitted," "What if he tells my parents?," "What if she medicates me and I get all groggy,"* etc.

The following are two cases that will help us reflect on some of the aspects that can influence the therapist when making a diagnosis.

CASE 1: *"I am a manipulator."*

This is a 28-year old patient diagnosed with BPD. She had previous diagnoses of anorexia and bulimia. She described herself as manipulative, a blackmailer, a liar and an endless number of negative labels about herself. When asked to describe what it meant to her to be manipulative and a blackmailer, she was very surprised and did not know what to say. After a while, she said, *"Well, that's what I've been told by psychologists who have seen me, that it was part of my disorder."* When querried about her manipulations, when she resorted to them, the reason, the results, etc., we concluded that the results were really very bad for her and that the manipulation was largely ineffective. The reason: what she had learned over time.

She had used this type of behavior for many years and had not considered that the result was almost always ineffective and harmful, since she would often end up attempting suicide or in situations that were very unpleasant and negative for her. Manipulation? Calls for attention? It could be. First of all, it is a way of asking for help. Maybe not the best, nor one that is expected by others, but it is a way of doing it: *Her* way of doing it.

Her mother was angry because her daughter left clues behind before her suicide attempts and described these in negative terms. It is sometimes difficult to understand that this is a way of asking for help. A first step towards the therapeutic work is to help the patient ask for help in a more effective and less harmful way. By exploring the reactions in the family, we observed that they were not helpful for generating changes in the patient. They usually responded with comments like: *"You're doing it again! You're calling for attention, you like to scare me shitless,"* etc.

Regarding the suicide attempts, the mother was not able to listen to her daughter or to the therapist. She just repeated herself over and over using different words: *"This (her daughter) has no solution,"* *"This is unbearable,"* *"I don't know what to do,"* *"This problem is incurable,"* *"I've tried everything, but nothing works."*

When she was given any suggestion, the answer was: *"I've already tried it."* It was strange, because she even answered before we had finished formulating the proposal.

Example of communication between them:

> Mother: *"She always comes to me when she tries to kill herself"* (with sarcasm and irony).
>
> Patient: *"Don't worry, the next time I won't come to you if it bothers you so much."*

In relation to the assessment, in this case there would have several possible interferences:

1. The information provided by the mother, who described her daughter as a manipulative person with many provocative and antisocial traits.
2. The information provided by the patient. *"I'm aggressive, I don't care about others, I use people, I manipulate therapists to get what I want, I hate men, if someone messes with me I am able to kill, people make me sick, I don't have any problems, I don't accept rules, if they tell me to do something, I do the opposite,"* etc.
3. Previous reports that included multiple diagnoses and comments such as: *"Fails to comply with rules,"* *"no empathy whatsoever,"* etc.

During the first interview, inconsistencies were observed between non-verbal language and reports from the patient, who seemed to have gathered a lot of information. When shown interest in knowing what lay beneath the defenses and behind that disgust toward people and her manipulations, the patient began to talk about a personal history full of abuse and neglect. The next day, there was a card in the office mailbox saying, *"Thank you for treating me like you did, I felt like a person, not just as a patient or a problem."*

In this case, the diagnosis was BPD, the patient was hypersensitive, with great capacity for empathy, great concern for others, great insecurity, many doubts, and felt *"burnt out from so many treatments and diagnosis."*

CASE 2: *"I have the feeling I have not explained myself very well."*

This is a 32-year-old male patient. He came in after a crisis, was nervous and defensive, but eager to know what was happening to him. He had read information on BPD and identified with it. His partner said that BPD accurately reflected him and corroborated many of the doubts he had about his difficulty verbalizing his feelings. A part of him did not want to have this disorder and refused to provide meaningful information to allow establishing a diagnosis. We provided additional tests, including a biographical questionnaire, the personality questionnaire SCID-II (structured interview for Axis II Personality Disorders), the Barratt Impulsiveness Scale (BIS-11), Seeking Sensations Scale (SSS), and Linehan's Reasons for Living Scale, and it appeared that he met the diagnostic criteria for BPD.

By delving into the questions from the questionnaires, he began to open up and offer more meaningful information than what he provided during the first interview. He stated that he had a hard time expressing his feelings and describing his problems and that, also, he did not want to assume he really has a problem. Yet, during the first four sessions, although he remained distant, apathetic, and uninterested, he kept coming back. During his vacation, he chose to go to another professional who misdiagnosed him with schizoid or schizotypal disorder.

When discussing what had happened, he says: *"I feel I have not explained myself very well, but, really, I have not lied."* He said that he did not expand on the answers he gave the other professional and did not know why, because he trusted the professional. However, in spite of feeling much respect for the professional, he had a sensation of being quite blocked. He stated feeling somewhat lost at the time of the visit and not well.

There are several factors in affecting an accurate diagnosis in this case:

1. The information omitted by the patient.
2. His desire to *"have something different"* and *"less crappy."*
3. His tendency to withdraw; his difficulty verbalizing what is happening to him, although he has the capacity to do so.
4. The feeling of insecurity toward a person he respects. This man always felt blocked when he had to talk about something important with his father.
5. Substance abuse. He gives conflicting information about whether he started consuming before or after the beginning of his problems.

This is another example of the importance of not basing our evaluations only on the data we receive and paying attention to what is not said and the information that does not fit in or is missing. If the patient appears distant and omits important information, it will be important to try and understand what lies underneath; hence the importance of having good training in psychotraumatology, attachment, and dissociation, and being aware of the most common relationship problems (Mosquera & González, 2009, 2011).

Finally, we must remember that a diagnosis should always be established by a professional and that we cannot rely on information contained in a chapter, an article, or a web page, since often other medical conditions such as dissociative disorders, attention deficit hyperactivity disorder in adults, bipolar disorder, or psychotic disorders may have similar presentations. It is essential not only to pay attention to external symptoms, but to fully understand the underlying process.

Chapter 10
Defense Mechanisms

Defense mechanisms are not diagnostic criteria, but occasionally, if their function is not understood, they can interfere and generate a lot of confusion in patients and the people they relate to, including therapists.

What are defense mechanisms?

Broadly speaking, we can say that they are certain responses (involving behaviors, thoughts and or emotions) to situations that the person has difficulty managing and involve many different feelings and sensations, such as anger, sadness, anxiety, frustration, and misunderstanding.

Usually, defense mechanisms are unconscious and although intended to relieve discomfort, they are often counterproductive and greatly interfere with people's quality of life. In moments of high intensity, people with borderline personality disorder (BPD) may come to perceive others as threats, even as potential enemies from whom they must protect themselves, and it is common for them to cope with situations and problems in a way that is sometimes difficult to understand. Feelings such as lack of confidence in oneself and conditions like vulnerability, hypersensitivity, lack of maturity, or experiences of previous failures may be factors that make people with BPD become extremely cautious or suspicious in order to protect themselves.

In the section of the *Rough Diamonds II* program (Mosquera, 2013b) dedicated to defense mechanisms, we make a distinction between those that are simple and complex. Examples of simple mechanisms are dichotomous thinking, projective identification, selective mood changes, magical thinking, denial, and lying or omitting information. Complex mechanisms include dissociation, which allows the blocking of emotionally intolerable memories or situations, and depersonalization, which makes people feel like observers of the world, disconnected from their emotional part and better able to handle the situation, although this feeling may be puzzling for the patients.

Providing psychoeducation about defense mechanisms can be very useful and may help people with BPD be aware of which mechanism/s they are using and the advantages or disadvantages these may have. Most of the time, patients are not aware of using them, and that is why there are often great discoveries in that section of the program. On one hand, it helps them understand some of the reasons why people around them may feel confused and how their reactions help misunderstandings arise. They begin to have a greater sense of control. When they pay attention and resort to more effective alternatives, they can stop and think about possible responses that may have better consequences for them and for their relatives.

Defense mechanisms in people with BPD can take multiple forms and nuances, but all are characterized by reaching high intensity in a very short period of time.

As mentioned in the introduction, people who use these mechanisms often do so unconsciously and may confuse the people around them, generating misunderstandings due to many of their reactions. In this sense, and during these people's individual treatments, it is important to make them more aware and help them replace these defensive reactions with more adaptive responses. This helps them start having a greater sense of control. When they pay attention and resort to more effective alternatives, they can handle situations with less emotional exhaustion, both when communicating and when working to resolve conflicts and deal with situations.

A simple defense mechanism would be **denial**: protection through avoiding an issue, refusing to talk about it, or ignoring it. An example would be: *"I don't go to the doctor in case he might find anything wrong with me."* Is it really useful to maintain this attitude? If the person has something wrong, the only way to treat it is to receive medical care. Sometimes, this is done with the hope that the discomfort will disappear on its own, so they do not look for or accept help. But the fact is that simply ignoring it will not make it go away. Denying reality or changing the subject when talking about something that affects them would be another example of how patients use this defense.

Another common defense mechanism is to focus on what is going wrong in one's life and not allow any room for possible solutions. The most characteristic example of this mechanism would be to answer **"Yes, but..."** to any proposed solution. This serves as protection against the risk of trying some kind of change in life, even when it may be for the better. This is an automatic mechanism and it is important to control it, because people who are trying to help may feel very frustrated to see that the person does not accept the help that is being offered. In some cases, patients who have used it unconsciously state having noticed that their friends have drifted away, their relatives have given up, and professionals thrown in the towel. This mechanism is closely related to one that has to do with lack of commitment to a decision, in which any attempt to carry it out is postponed and becomes a **self-fulfilling prophecy.** That is, they think that whichever path they choose is not going to be positive and they look for the negative aspects in order not to move forward. Thus, that purpose will never be achieved because fear of failure, or not accepting the consequences of whatever choice they make, will make the person focus exclusively on the chances that everything will go wrong, or at least not as they would like. This would be an example of "closing the doors on oneself."

Dichotomous thinking, "all-or-nothing," or what some authors call thinking in terms of black-and-white, is a mechanism in which the nuances or gray areas are very difficult to perceive and, therefore, virtually impossible to take into account. The person moves between extremes and is unable to perceive a middle ground. An example would be: *"Either I accurately and completely get what I want, or it's not worth anything."* It is important to clarify that this usually happens when the person is emotionally activated, since in times of stability they are usually able to reach intermediate conclusions or positions.

Another simple defense mechanism would be **selective mood changes.** Obviously, mood changes cannot always be controlled and generally relate to something that has happened. But there are times when people learn that by getting angry they can put an end to any demands from others or the possibility that someone will argue with them (not hearing something they do not like), or that by crying, arguments stop. This mechanism is usually associated with learning, because in many cases, emotionally colorful responses receive immediate attention and have been reinforced by relatives for a while. Let us see some examples:

> Example 1: *"You're right, I've noticed that if I ask for something in a loving way, I get it and then everything is as tense as usual. I feel manipulative and very guilty for hurting my family, but I cannot help not getting along with them."*
>
> Example 2: *"Sometimes, I try to express how I feel, but it doesn't work, I feel ignored. But when I scream, when I get angry, or I get sad, they make more efforts to understand me. Then I feel terrible, but it works, I don't know how to do it otherwise."*

Magical thinking, as discussed in Chapter 2, is another defense mechanism that can often be seen in those affected by this diagnosis. It is when patients think that a person, place, thing, or idea is able to make problems instantly disappear or make them feel happy and safe. That feeling is something like *"if I have or get _____, I will feel good."*

Magical thinking is that something is going to make everything happen according to what they desire, and that the world or others are responsible for repairing all the bad moments that have happened. Although this thought seem logical or desirable, it usually brings about frustration, discomfort, and feeling like throwing in the towel, since whatever is desired or expected will not happen with magic solutions. Here's an example:

> *"I always thought my problems would be solved by having a car, I would be more motivated, I would go to more places, and I would relate to more people, but when I bought the car, I felt much worse because nothing happened as I had expected."*

These types of thoughts, that imply that difficulties and solutions are due to external elements and that these elements will be able to fully or partially turn their life around, are thoughts that patients can hold onto at certain times as the only alternative to solving their problems. In this case, dreaming and becoming excited about these goals seems to help, but we believe magical thinking needs to be addressed in order to attribute control and responsibility to patients, not to external elements. We must help them focus on realistic goals that depend on them and not on magical solutions or other people.

Another common defense mechanism is **procrastination/postponing**. It is used when they are not sure which is the best decision, or when carrying it out would pose a considerable effort they do not want to make or for which they do not feel prepared. The issue is that this only increases discomfort, because the problem or difficulty remains unresolved. And though at times it may be useful (e.g., postponing a conversation if one is not calm enough to speak productively), at other times it can be very harmful.

Finally, in regards to simple defense mechanisms, we should mention that people with this diagnosis often use **projection** when they feel insecure, believe thay are incapable of doing something something, or when they feel frustrated, attacked, or questioned. The reaction is usually unconscious and rather impulsive, and what is verbalized may be very different from what they actually mean or feel, so they get the feeling that they are misinterpreted or not understood. Sometimes, patients may be convinced of what they are saying because at the time of distress they may actually be thinking that, and what they do is project their discomfort on the world, the injustices, the defects, the mistakes, and the difficulties of others, or anything else external to themselves so as not to take responsibility for what is happening to them.

It is something like "*it bounces off of me and explodes on you.*" Projective identification allows people to get rid of their discomfort and whatever is causing it and place it outside themselves. It is as if they could transfer their negative thoughts, doubts, and insecurities onto other people.

> Example: *"If someone says something about me, although initially it may not be negative, I begin to question the other person and suddenly I find myself using it against them."*

This mechanism generates confusion in those who perceive it, since relatives often comment things like "*sometimes a gesture or a look is enough.*" There are relatives who feel that they are being attacked just for looking. This may be due to the fact that people with BPD tend to see what they think of themselves, or what they think others think, reflected in that look, as explained by the following example:

> Example: Patient lying on the couch thinking he is useless and wasting his days. When the father enters the room, he says, *"What you looking at? Do you want to take my picture? You can be proud of your son. You've turned your son in a perfectly useless guy. Now you can go and tell everyone: I am proud, I got my son to be a useless person."*

Dissociation, depersonalization and derealization are also defense mechanisms, but are more complex than those mentioned so far. Both can produce some disconnection from reality, so that people may not even remember what they are experiencing due to the intensity of the moment. They may end up feeling really terrible because these experiences are perceived as strange and may even lead them to believe they are going crazy. In fact, there will be times when they will completely forget an argument, or the reason for it, and they may give the impression that they are lying to ignore issues that are difficult to handle; but the fact is that they will actually be unable to remember them.

When it is an issue with which patients cannot deal, it can generate a blockage of information that becomes dissociated. That is, they do not have access to this information; it remains stored in a hidden compartment of the brain. This could explain some of the reactions from the patients (observing their disconnection, having difficulty remembering important events, or having very vague memories of situations that other people who were present remember perfectly well, etc.).

Depersonalization and derealization is often verbalized by patients with comments such as, *"Sometimes I feel that I am disconnected from my body," "I feel that the world is not real," "It's like I am seeing myself from afar."*

Dissociation can be defined as the loss of contact with reality when a person is conscious. It is not usually a psychotic experience. It is like being somewhere else within the mind, somewhere other than where they are physically, forgetting things that happened just a few days or hours ago and that others remember perfectly well, trying to focus on something that is happening in the present moment and not being able to do so, having the feeling of having been to other places, and even waking up wearing clothes that they do not remember putting on or buying.

There are mild forms of absorption similar to dissociation that almost all people have experienced at some point. For example, holding a conversation and not being aware of what has been said, riding on a train, bus, or car and not remembering what happened along the way (without falling asleep), or taking notes in class while thinking about other things. However, there are other more serious forms of dissociation, such as allowing abusive contact from another person without being fully aware of what is happening. In this case, it serves as a defense mechanism, a way to disconnect from something that is hurtful to the person.

Some authors think that it is more likely that people who dissociate have suffered some form of abuse in childhood and that this, in turn, is related to self-harm. They say that self-destructive behaviors usually have a component of numbness for the person. Sometimes, it is a response to a feeling, image, or sound that reminds them of something painful or traumatic. In some cases, it is as if the person needed to find a way out when emotions become too intense and overwhelming to bear as we mentioned in Chapter 9 on dissociation.

If we consider these defense mechanisms and try to remember that they are exactly that, the patients´ way of defending themselves, it is much more likely that we will not end up burned out or overwhelmed by the difficulty of some cases and, above all, that we will not respond with countertransference reactions that can harm our patients. We will be looking at countertransference issues in detail in the following chapter.

Chapter 11
Countertransference and Borderline Personality Disorder

"We suspect that the words 'difficult patient' and 'borderline' are synonymous in the minds of many mental health professionals. We can go further and assume that the borderline personality disorder diagnosis is often based on how difficult a person is... It should be clear at this point that we do not consider all difficult patients to be borderlines or all borderlines to be difficult. Many borderlines are difficult, many are not; anyway, we must treat them whether they are difficult or not... "

Wessler, Hankin, & Stern (2001)

"What makes us feel uncomfortable with the borderline person's pressure is not the patient himself, but we ourselves... in the treatment of borderline personality disorder and other severe personality disorders, what is most dangerous is our own character."

Lewin & Schulz (1992)

"The reasons why borderlines are such difficult therapy cases do not reside exclusively on the patients... Therapists get into therapeutic difficulties because they respond to the pathology of the borderlines, although this is only partly true. Therapists are struggling with their own problems, blind spots, and ways of being, as well as with lack of information or inadequate training."

Jerome Kroll (1988)

Many people with Borderline Personality Disorder (BPD) have great difficulties observing personal boundaries and those of others. This includes therapists.

Often, they have great ability and ingenuity to drive professionals crazy. Therapists find themselves taking calls after-hours, lengthening sessions, and offering special treatment they do not usually give to other patients. This is due to countertranference. That is the emotional responses generated in professionals who treat them.

When professionals feel manipulated, used, coerced by patients, or responsible for their moods, it may be a case that is generating countertrasference. To discover how we are being driven by the patient's reactions, and in a way, making them ours is certainly disconcerting.

As Gabbard and Wilkinson (2000) state in the introduction of their book *Management of countertransference with borderline patients*, in few disorders could we devote an entire volume to the emotional reactions that those who suffer them generate in the professionals who serve them.

Therefore, it is not uncommon to find professionals who refuse to serve these people and who refer to them as tending to burn-out therapists. Certainly, some people with this diagnosis have great ability to drive us nuts. They are known to possess a special intuition to perceive weaknesses and this can be very uncomfortable for the therapist.

In addition, we can talk about professionals who act too critical and too directive, showing intolerance, anger, disappointment, or frustration because the patient does not improve enough. For many patients these interventions or attitudes prevent the creation of a good therapeutic alliance and have a very negative effect on prognosis. Let us not forget the emotional harm we can do to them. Another less harmful alternative for both, especially for the patient, who is the person we are interested in, is to take these behaviors for what they are and work on them. They are simply ways to cope with discomfort and because they can interfere with therapy, working them out will strengthen the therapeutic alliance and the patient's trust. Therapists need to maintain a position of flexibility, adaptability, and unconditional acceptance so that their interventions can retain therapeutic maneuverability.

COMMON COUNTERTRANSFERENCE FEELINGS AND REACTIONS: ANXIETY, FEAR, INSECURITY AND/OR FEAR

Regardless of what happens in the course of therapy, these patients can easily make therapists feel anxious. Fear of suicide and challenges to the therapist are often present, especially in the first sessions. Saying the wrong word or using an inadequate tone of voice or look may make the patient react aggressively, attempt suicide, self-injure, or leave slamming the door behind and not return. For example, when a patient says, *"People who are afraid make me sick,"* while falling silent and staring at you.

Feeling Blackmailed

Therapists can feel emotionally blackmailed by patients' suicide threats. For example, when a patient says, *"I thought you were different and you really worried about what happened to me. I see you're just like everyone else. Don't worry, I know what I'll do tonight..."*

Feelings of Guilt

Therapists can feel guilty about the deterioration of the therapy, such as when the patient does not progress, is not constant, does not bring homework, self-injures, etc. For example, when a patient says, *"I've taken the pills because I called you at 3 a.m. and your phone was turned off."*

Rescue Fantasies

Therapists can feel as if they must do things for the patients. They may even think they are the only ones who can help the patient. For example, when a patient says, *"You're the only person who can help me and understand me, if it wasn't for you, I wouldn't be alive."*

Feeling of Not Being Worthy or Being a Fraud

Patients with BPD tend to question the therapist's competence. For example, when a patient says: *"This case is too much for you. Admit that you do not know how to treat me and let's get this farce over with."*

Feeling Invaded

The therapist perceive that the patient is trying to invade their privacy and to confuse the therapeutic relationship. An example is when the patient says, *"We always talk about me. Do you have a partner or children? Next time we can meet in a restaurant."*

WHERE CAN THIS TAKE US?

- Not to want to treat these people.
- To blame patients for our inability to help them.
- To collaborate in the low social acceptance and bad press they often receive.

In short, as therapists we may use our own defense mechanisms and think in terms of: *"It's normal for them to leave therapy, dropout statistics are very high," "These patients are difficult"* ...

All this can lead us to a final countertransference reaction: the transgression of professional boundaries. Therapists can believe that if they do not do what patients demand, they will hurt themselves and, instead of remaining true to their principles, they yield to the patients' unreasonable demands, which is not helpful for the patient or the therapy. Relinquishing professional boundaries interacts with all of the above. The professional, in addition to feeling blackmailed may experience fear, anxiety, guilt, or feel responsible for the patient's outcome.

Given the above, we have various alternatives. Among them is switching gears: turning established assumptions around. Simply understanding these behaviors and trying to see them and cope with them in a more flexible way can greatly facilitate our work. This will help us avoid responding with countertransference reactions that, as mentioned before, can greatly harm patients and, of course, precipitate a sudden dropout from therapy. See some alternatives in the table on the next page.

EXAMPLES OF ALTERNATIVES

	THEORY/ASSUMPTION	ALTERNATIVE
PROJECTION	A **defense mechanism** that these people often use to distance themselves from a part of themselves that they do not want or do not like and which they attribute to someone else.	**This is an attempt at communication** by patients. It aims to make therapists understand them, making them feel what they feel. This can help us understand their fears.
BOUNDARIES	**Rigid boundaries** • They do not respect the professionals' boundaries. • You have to be extra careful with these manipulative people. • They do it to annoy you. *"I bet he thinks he is my only patient."* • It is essential to set firm boundaries (schedules, calls, etc.). Certain behaviors should not be allowed.	**Flexible boundaries** • We do not respect the patients' limitations. • We have to be extra careful with these people who are so sensitive. • They are not aware of how their behavior affects others. • We should understand transgression of established boundaries as relevant information about how this person acts in real life.
SELF-HARM	**Calls for attention** Actions: • Disarm the person: Remove knives and sharp objects from the house, removing medication, sleep with the person to prevent suicide… • Tell the family that if they don't control the person at all times *"they will end up killing themselves."*	**Calls for help** Actions: • The best weapon is trusting the person. No drastic measures. Reach agreements and give responsibility. Do not invalidate. Just try to avoid the availability of means (removing medication, sharp objects, etc.) in very acute crises. • Take the blame off the family. Help them assume that, if a person wants to commit suicide, they will end up doing so, although there is always the possibility of avoiding it and, therefore, it is important to try.

Besides taking all this into account, if at any given time professionals feel the need to disclose things to the patient, the best we can do is first reflect internally, not get carried away by the intensity of the moment, and consider the possibility of seeking supervision.

It is important to bear in mind that people with BPD, who have sought treatment from other professionals and have been hopping from one therapist to the next for years without results, often come in feeling burned-out, lacking energy and confidence and, therefore, they may adopt a defensive position that should not be surprising. In any case, we should not take this personally, but instead see it as one of the problems for which the patient needs our help.

Poor adherence to treatment in people with BPD, in most cases, is a myth and not a reality, so to end this chapter, here are some questions that we, as professionals, should ask ourselves when our interventions do not work with so many people.

Is it possible that we are the ones who are doing something wrong? Why, when something does not work on so many people, does it continue to be applied? Can this help those affected or is it perhaps a way to corroborate the bad results we already know about? Could this intervention be a professional defense mechanism due to our inability to reach these people? Is it possible that at times we may not even consider asking those who truly are experts on this subject what may or may not be helpful?

Part Four
Treatment

Chapter 12
The Importance of Medication as a Complement to the Treatment of BPD

Although there is no specific medication for borderline personality disorder (BPD), there are certain pharmacological drugs that can help manage specific symptoms. Medication may, for example:

- Reduce anxiety
- Reduce depressive symptoms and irritability
- Control impulses (including self-mutilation)
- Correct misinterpretations of reality

In short, medication may help with mood regulation and stabilization, thus increasing accessibility to the patient, provided they are not over-medicated.

First of all, it is essential that physicians address these issues. When we think that someone may need or may benefit from medication, we should refer them to a specialist in psychiatry for an evaluation. Sometimes patients prefer to ask their therapists about their opinion on medication and its adjustments by their psychiatrists. It is a tricky situation, because we should neither ignore the issue, nor invade another professional's field of expertise. In an ideal situation, we would build a team of professionals, so that both psychologist and psychiatrist could regularly communicate with each other.

Sometimes, metaphors can be used to explain certain issues related to medication:

> "Recovery is like crossing a bridge. In order to get to the other side, it's important to know the bridge, to know where it can take you, and why you want to cross it. Although this may be very clear to you, there are issues such as impulsivity (attempting to cross the bridge by jumping) that may make your goal quite difficult to achieve. Well, medication stabilizes you while you are crossing and until you get to the other side. It helps you see things more clearly and be more attentive to directions or suggestions from a possible therapy."

That is, medication can stabilize the person and/or decrease their emotional rollercoaster, but medication alone is not enough. Nevertheless, it is an almost essential partner in therapy in many BPD cases.

According to Gunderson (2002), the basic purpose of medication is to reduce subjective distress (i.e., symptoms that patients consider undesirable) and help contain behavioral problems, often considered undesirable by others and, in most cases, by patients themselves. He also notes that, although drugs are often useful in the treatment of these patients, the role of medication in the long-term care of borderline patients remains unclear. In some cases, medication helps improve symptoms. And, for many physicians, it seems increasingly clear that there is an important biological component.

It is essential to remind patients that they must be consistent with medication in order to notice and obtain results, usually after a minimum of 2 to 4 weeks. The body needs an adjustment period to many medications. We can help reinforce consistency in medication intake by informing patients about potential benefits, adverse effects, and the risk of sudden relapses if taken only (or suddenly discontinued) in moments of crisis. In addition, responsible use of medication is the only way to assess its effectiveness.

As mentioned before, medication can help ensure that patients are more receptive to therapy and obtain more benefits from psychological treatment. But we should not recommend that they take it or influence their decision in any way. Instead, we should answer their questions to the extent that we can, talk about cases in which medication may be helpful, and let them know that doctors are those who can inform them more precisely about the potential benefits and disadvantages. Psychiatric doctors can talk to them about why they believe medication will be helpful, possible side effects of each drug (although this must be done carefully with people who are very suggestible), and/or alternative medication. As professionals, we should all try to stand in the patient's shoes and ask ourselves if we would take medication without any explanation or perhaps just vague explanations such as, *"it's the best thing you can do," "it's recommended in these cases," "without medication there is no solution".* All these reasons may make sense in certain contexts, but we must adapt them to the patient. There are patients who prefer not to know what they are taking and just follow directions without objection. Even so, a brief explanation is always appropriate.

CASE EXAMPLE: *"I thought I was going to die."*

Let us take the case of a patient who never asked any questions about her medication. She just wrote down what she had to take, when, and how frequently. A few months ago, her doctor changed her medication. She did not complain and started the new medicine. She began to feel dizzy, strange, and confused, as if she were somewhere else. Then she began to pass out and forget small things that happened before she fainted. She started to become afraid of leaving the house alone in case it happened again.

After a week of screenings and assessments, and after ruling out sudden epilepsy, the problem was finally discovered. It was a side effect of the new medication. She thought that the above symptoms were new effects of her condition and that, for some unknown reason, her discomfort now presented in that way. At no point had she thought it could be a side effect of the new medication.

Now we remember this episode as an anecdote, but the story could have had a very different ending. Luckily, this young woman had made good improvements on her self-harm issues, but if this had happened at a different time, perhaps just a few months before, she could have overdosed again in order to end the discomfort she was feeling.

Some patients with borderline personality disorder have to choose whether to endure the side effects of medication in addition to the intrinsic symptoms of the disorder. Some face the reality of medication being an added problem in their lives, but it can others the chance of achieving greater peace of mind and making better use of psychotherapy. Taking individual situations into consideration is crucial: Every patient is unique both from a biological and a temperamental perspective and this will inevitably affect the possible effects of medication. Many patients greatly benefit from pharmacological treatment, provided that it is administered as prescribed by the psychiatrist. Sometimes patients and their families complain about the uselessness of medication, but if we inquire about medication intake, we often find many deficiencies. In order to assess the effectiveness of any medication, we must follow the indications of the prescription and, of course, avoid drug and/or alcohol use, which can reduce or alter the effects of these drugs.

In regards to medication, those of us who are psychotherapists or psychologists and do not prescribe usually work daily with many patients who complain about medication as well as others who will take anything even if they do no notice any effects just because the doctor said so. We should not try to cover matters that are beyond our expertise and training, but instead surround ourselves with good professionals with whom we can consult. This way, we can refer to a psychiatrist those patients who are willing to take medication and who we believe may benefit from it, so their need for psychopharmacological treatment can be evaluated.

Many patients feel dependent on medication; other become tired because they really do not notice any results, since their suffering and other problems continue to be present; nevertheless, others do notice changes and improvement, but this improvement does not outweigh some of the side effects. One common problem among girls, for example, is overweight. Some say that medication helps, but the side effects make them feel even worse. The following testimony is from a person who does notice the positive effects of medication, but for whom the negative side effects are more noticeable:

> "I think you know I always do what professionals tell me to do, I've never refused to take medication despite the bad experiences I've had. Initially, I never reject medication and I always give it a try. You know I used to feel bad and had many ups and downs. Now you can say I'm a little bit calmer, I don't get so obsessive, and I'm not so impulsive. But if I already felt bad about myself before, now I gross myself out, I don't recognize my body. What I'm saying may perhaps seem frivolous, but if in order to treat one problem I have to face another one, I don't know which one I prefer. I don't mind gaining a few kilos, but I've gained 17."

> *"This means not only being overweight and rejecting my body, but also discomfort, lack of agility, tiredness, and buying new clothes because nothing fits anymore, not even my underwear, the only thing that still fits are my socks. This, coupled with the high prices of medication is placing me in a financial position that is becoming increasingly difficult to sustain. Do you understand what I mean? Is this 'stability' really worth it? Before, at least I got out of the house, but now I'm ashamed; you know how people can be very intrusive and I'm sick of the expressions of surprise and questions like 'But what happened to you?'"*

In this case, we can see how the side effects worsen the initial situation. Consequently, this patient opted for changing her treatment and immersing herself more intesively in psychotherapy and the result was ultimately much more effective. As she gained weight, she felt more and more unmotivated, which makes sense, given that the physical change was exaggerated and she no longer looked like the same person.

Many patients give medication a chance and try to follow the directions when they receive explanations about why a particular prescription drug will be useful. But when they do not receive any explanation or relevant information is omitted, they may stop taking the medication at the smallest setback, often without consulting their doctor.

The role of the psychologist, who sees the patient much more often, in such cases can be very helpful, so it is important to work together as a team. It is important to encourage them to address their complaints directly with their psychiatrist, because this will enable them to seek alternatives in order to solve these problems. There are also some cases in which the side effects are desirable, such as when some people find out that a certain medication makes them lose weight and they increase the dose without talking to the doctor, or when a prescription drug prevents them from thinking, so they resort to it in order not to feel. In these cases, side effects are well received. Obviously, in all of these cases, what seems to be a problem may be workable if the patient trusts the therapeutic process enough and we have access to this information.

The therapeutic work usually flows much better with patients who are not excessively medicated. It is very difficult to treat a person who is falling asleep and can barely keep up with the conversation. In these cases, a second psychiatric opinion is always recommended, since these are often patients who have been in psychiatric treatment for years with widely spaced follow-up sessions and whose medication has been increased along the way or other medications added due to the fact that they do not seem to get better. However, this very much depends on the case and the prescribing psychiatrist.

Case: *"I am not getting my period"*

This is a 24-year-old patient with emotional instability. She has been in psychopharmacological treatment for two years without any changes and has not been given any explanations. She states she is swollen up, has gained a lot of weight, and is not getting her period, so she feels very uncomfortable. When asked if she had discussed this with her psychiatrist she said she had, but he did not consider it important and told her he was not going to make any changes. The patient decided to seek a second opinion and the new doctor began to gradually reduce the medication she was taking and recommended a new prescription drug cocktail for treating her symptoms. The new doctor specified the reasons for taking each medication and their potential effects. The psychiatrist not only informed her about the possible side effects that she might notice, but also asked her to call him if she happened to experience a number of symptoms. This provided reassurance to the patient and gave her a sense of control and trust in the doctor. With the change, the patient began to feel much better, livelier, with increased attention span, and much less swollen. This helped her find enough motivation to start making positive changes in her life and greatly facilitated her therapeutic work.

In short, medication can become a facilitator for change or interfere with our work and our patients' ability to regain control of their life. Patients who are medicated in excess may not retain or assimilate the information or the guidelines we offer them in therapy, or at least not in the same way they could if they were taking medication tailored to their actual needs. Sometimes patients are bothersome and this can lead some doctors to overly medicate them.

One patient came to the first interview completely unmotivated, sleepy, slow, and had great difficulty following the conversation. At first, the therapist thought she might be a person with very limited intellectual capacity and thought adapting to her rhythm would be necessary. Sessions were very long and slow, both for therapist and patient. In the third session, she decided to go to another psychiatrist for a second opinion; with the new doctor the patient felt understood, heard, and well taken care of. The therapist was greatly surprised in the following session, because the person who came in had nothing in common with the young woman who had atended the previous sessions. When the patient had been talking for a while about her news and how she felt with this new treatment, the therapist decided to disclose her previous impression, because she thought that even if the patient were half asleep, she would be aware that the psychoeducational materials given to her had been very much simplified.

> Therapist: *"I'm pleasantly surprised; in addition to noticing that you are more awake and lively, I get the impression that you feel you have the control of what you say and think."*

> Patient: (Smiles.) *"I feel better. With the medication I could not think, it was a tremendous effort, everything was very difficult."*

> T : *"I hope you did not feel misunderstood in previous sessions, I had doubts about your ability to follow conversations and I was under the impression that I had to greatly simplify the answers."*
>
> C : *"I understand perfectly, you probably thought I was dumb."*
>
> T: *"I absolutely did not think you were dumb, but I thought you had some limitations and many difficulties in focusing your attention and following the explanations."* (At the end of each session, the patient requested a quick summary, because she did not remember what had been discussed. She asked the therapist to write down on a card what she was expected to do during the week so she could try to do it.)
>
> C : *"I couldn't, I was totally incapacitated, numb; but you can see that I am not dumb at all; just a little bit, but it went away when they readjusted my medication."* (The patient laughs.)
>
> T : *"What do you think about reviewing the goals we initially set?"*
>
> C : (Nods.) *"You know? I've been thinking about all the lost time and have made several decisions."* (The patient fluently continues with the conversation.)

In this case, excessive medication limited the patient, interfering with her ability to think, retain information, communicate, and listen.

In this case, medication was a tremendous interference and did not facilitate the possibility of change at all. In addition to obstructing the patient's quality of life and her control of many basic functions, it interfered with her ability to benefit from psychotherapy. The worst part was not the difficulties in themselves, but the ideas that a poorly medicated patient can generate and believe such as *"she will always be this way"* and *"it's not worth living like this."* Sadly, this is how it is in many cases.

To conclude this chapter, it should be said that in most cases, medication that prescribed with adequate communication with the patient and is properly adjusted and adapted to the patient's symptoms can be vey helpful and does not have to generate side effects that interfere with the patient's quality of life. Medication can be stabilizing and greatly facilitate the state of concentration and attention needed to integrate the resources and skills worked on in psychotherapy and can also help reduce discomfort and psychological distress.

Chapter 13
Group Therapy

One of the basic goals of group therapy for people with this diagnosis is for participants to become aware of how their ways of communicating and behaving affects others and to be able to observe how, in turn, other people affect them. Group therapy offers opportunities for psychoeducation and building coping skills. Participating in a group can help them improve communication and express feelings appropriately. Another goal is to help them understand how other people with similar problems act and suffer, since this allows them to see themselves reflected in the behavior and reactions of their peers.

Some people with borderline personality disorder believe it is better not to share their feelings with others because they may not be understood. As discussed in Chapter 6, such beliefs are often related to past negative experiences of having their feelings or opinions invalidated and/or judged. At times, this affects them so much that some choose to avoid contact with other people and completely isolate themselves in the most extreme cases, thinking that by doing so things will be less complicated.

In these cases, attending a group can be very positive, as it can help them understand that isolating and avoiding relationships with others does not allow them to put new alternative coping skills into practice. Isolation can be positive at certain moments, but more as an exceptional strategy that allows them to take time to reflect on what happened before reaching conclusions. Problems arise when this time of withdrawal lengthens and becomes the patient's habitual way of coping with problems in interpersonal relations: the more they isolate, the more difficult it becomes to resume contact with others.

As mentioned before, many people with BPD fear other people's reactions. They fear that other people may be surprised, disgusted, disappointed, or critical of their feelings. However, when they join group therapy and they feel understood and not judged, the result is a great sense of relief. Assuring supportive interactions and freedom from negative judgements are aspects that can be controlled in group therapy. Sharing with others gives group therapy participants the opportunity to discuss their feelings and allows them to see the situation from different perspectives.

> *"I felt free, unbiased and, for the first time, I was able to express what I felt without barriers. I don't want to wear masks and here I'm just me, with my good and bad moments. When there are misunderstandings, we clear them up and nothing happens. Shared pain is easier to bear, it's just the honest-to-God truth and it has helped me improve in almost all of my issues, especially in communication."*

"What I liked the most about group therapy is meeting people who are going and have gone through the same stuff as me."

"In therapy, group sessions are essential for me; I really don't know how things would have been without them. Since I meet wonderful people there and feel useful, I've learned that this illness can happen to anyone, that it's not a punishment for being terrible."

"Therapy has helped me know myself better. I deeply value my participation in the group; knowing that there are others like me and I'm not a strange or unique being on this planet has helped me tremendously. I don't know when the group will end, but I will be very sad when that happens because it has helped me understand many things. Besides, my colleagues are very special and extraordinary people. They make me feel at ease, comfortable, integrated, and accepted. It's very difficult to explain. In most of the sessions we learn things that help us know ourselves better and also to relate to others in a healthier way. I even like misunderstandings because they help us rectify and learn not to make the same mistakes.

"I like the fact that we all participate and tell each other things, even personal stuff. It decreases my huge fear of rejection."

"Group members are nice people, no doubt due to their fine sensibilities. Emotions are very positive: solidarity, tenderness, joy, etc."

"The group gives me a sense of freedom, usefulness, empathy, complicity, and trust that is hard to find elsewhere. For me, it's a commitment to myself, to you, and to the group participants. I usually feel quite well in the meetings due to the atmosphere of trust, sincerity, and understanding that is created. What I like best is that there is an exchange of experiences with such a degree of trust and transparency, so difficult to achieve outside the group setting, that it turns the group into something unique, special, and positive. What I like least is the pain of others, I feel powerless, I do what I can and what I know in order to mitigate it, but I don't have a miracle potion, not for me or for anyone. I am very sensitive to the pain of others."

"The main reason I stay in the group is to enjoy the company of all my colleagues. I appreciate them all, I love to listen to them. The only thing that bothers me is that I never have any advice to give or words of encouragement in their lowest moments, and also the fact that my colleagues hold themselves in such low esteem, when I, and I say this objectively, consider them to be very special people, not at all 'mediocre,' 'monsters,' or 'worms' as they sometimes call themselves."

It is important for groups to focus on solutions and alternatives (to avoid turning them into venting groups, because participants can be harmed).

Sharing means being clear about what one feels, but also listening to the person who is listening to us. Some people tend to give long monologues about what happened as a way of venting, but usually the person does not feel better afterwards; the problem tends to remain present and one is not able to focus on solutions. It is necessary to clarify and understand the difference between sharing and venting, since it usually affects the way we interact with others.

In groups, we must explain that communication must be a two-way street. There are people who merely express complaint after complaint and leave few alternatives to the listener, since any suggestion will be answered with another complaint or a *"yes, but..."* One of the main reasons why groups are often helpful is the benefit of being able to listen and learn from the experiences of others who are experiencing or have experienced very similar problems. This involves listening to and respecting each one of the participants, since this will be the only way the group can become a safe environment in which each and every person can talk freely without fear of being judged, criticized, or invalidated. The latter are not tolerated in groups, because aside from being an interference, it can harm the people who attend the meetings.

It is important to teach patients to be selective when it comes to sharing feelings and thoughts. They need to understand that, due to the intensity with which they live emotions and situations, they have a tendency to expose themselves too much and the result is usually not positive. Their habitual way to share feelings and ask for help has often been intense, desperate, and unclear, and in many cases they expected others to rescue them or know exactly what they need. For this reason, it is necessary to help them see that it is important to be cautious when sharing intimate feelings and do it very gradually. The person we are confiding in may respond in an unexpected way and this could trigger negative reactions, and they must learn that the response from others will depend partially on how their way of sharing is perceived. Family and friends sometimes judge feelings or actions by saying that *"it's for your own good"* or *"it's with good intentions."* Their intentions may be good and constructive, but the end result may be harmful for the patient; therefore, these and other aspects are addressed in group sessions.

We all have bad moments, no one is always happy. We all worry about things, we get fed up, we feel exhausted, and this is normal. One of the goals of group therapy is to learn to handle these concerns in an effective way that does not worsen the situation or what one is feeling. Many patients with this diagnosis have difficulty managing emotions when they are intensely activated, generally after a disappointment or when something bad and unexpected happens. In these situations, people tend to get stuck on the negative emotion, which then grows and grows until they feel they are going to explode.

Discussing everyday concerns and seeing how others are coping with the same problems can help them understand and/or remember that they are not "weirdos." Specifically, they can learn how others are coping with similar problems and how, inadvertently, they themselves avoid establishing the personal relationships they would like to maintain.

It is easier to understand or recognize problems when we see them in others and this may help them understand or recognize their own difficulties. One of the main goals is to create an alliance between group members, a sense of belonging and teamwork, as well as helping them understand that this is a support group in which we will try to increase positive feelings between participants and strengthen and/or develop new skills to cope with everyday problems. In addition to this, another objective is to reduce the perception of being different that many of these patients have and, if in case they actually believe they are different, to conclude that each person is unique and different, not just them.

People with emotional instability often establish relationships that are intense, demanding and may end up being negative, unsatisfactory, and superficial. In the group they are given an opportunity to learn different (less intense), more adaptive (sharing task, alternatives, and solutions) and more satisfying ways of relating.

Group therapy helps us visualize both the positive and negative aspects of how each participant communicates and/or interacts with others. Being able to see this and point it out helps them learn from others and from the feedback of peers and therapists.

In order to get participants interested, assisting, and involved in therapy sessions, it is important to take into consideration the following points:

- Provide structure for group: let participants know what to expect from others, both peers and therapists, and what is expected of them. In this sense, it is often useful to spend part of the first session reviewing and/or creating a set of suggestions or norms to be observed during the sessions, in which continued attendance and active participation are key. Among these suggestions, the most common are deciding the length of the sessions, their frequency, how contacts are to be established outside of the group so they don´t interfere, etc. One of the basic rules of the group is confidentiality.
- Create a pleasant, safe environment.
- Allow participants to express themselves naturally, just as they do in daily life. Only then will we have access to their actual way of communicating and be able to help them change those aspects that may be interfering with their relationships with other people and with conflict resolution and/or misunderstandings.
- Take into account and request the participants' suggestions; ask for their opinion; this increases the feeling of teamwork.
- Address problems openly and give feedback to participants: frictions and misunderstandings are inevitable between group participants. When this happens, it is recommended that they be addressed in the same therapy session, since it is an excellent opportunity to practice the skills we want to teach in the groups. This is real life experience that misunderstandings can be resolved by talking.

- Promote the exchange of opinions: this helps create a safe environment in which each participant knows that they can and are expected to voice their opinion and that every suggestion will be heard and valued by all.

To create a safe environment in which they can talk about each one of their doubts is crucial. Once this is achieved, participants can rehearse ways to solve a potential conflict through role-playing. This allows them to become aware of the ways in which many of their reactions and behaviors interfere in their quality of life and in that of the people around them. They discover how effective communication can help them manage a situation and how its absence can worsen it. It also generates a mirror effect in which participants can see themselves reflected in others and learn from this reflection, perceiving both positive and negative aspects so they can change them.

Group therapy is an excellent complement to individual therapy. Many of the changes that occur are due to recognizing that other participants are people with similar symptoms, so perceptions of being weird or different usually decrease.

The group setting provides an opportunity to give and receive constructive feedback, not judgment or criticism, and this allows participants to learn to be more independent in their daily lives. The learning obtained in group therapy results in an increase in each participant's resources and skills, which over time are generalized until they become automatic.

Chapter 14
Family Therapy

People with borderline personality disorder (BPD) often have difficulties in relationships in general; difficulties which can intensify in their relationships with family members. Sometimes, due to exhaustion and wear caused by years of concern, their own relatives can adopt behaviors that are similar to those of the patient. Sometimes they do this as a desperate measure, *"to see if she realizes how I feel when she does that."* Other family reactions can serve as a psychological defense. Believing that people with BPD act this way because that is what they want can be easier than understanding that a loved one has a real problem, especially when the problem interferes and covers so many areas of these people's life and those who live with them (Mosquera, Ageitos, Bello, & Pitarch, 2009).

As dedicated professionals, we know first-hand that people with BPD may react disproportionately to situations that seem unimportant and even irrelevant. This, unfortunately, does not simplify our work with the individual or the family. If sometimes patients themselves have trouble understanding many of their own reactions, imagine the relatives who live daily with these people and end up becoming emotionally infected. Patients have their own responsibility, professionals have theirs; but, what about the family? What role do they play? For years, it was relatively common for the patient to come alone to therapy and to keep family members uninvolved. This was sometimes frustrating for parents, partners, or children, since they tried to find guidance or guidelines, but what they often received was criticism or silence. Fortunately, this is changing, and in recent years, the family is acquiring an important role in the intervention, as it had previously, but in the past the family was almost exclusively viewed as the cause of the problem (Mosquera, 2006). Family work is necessary, and in some cases, such as when patients live with or are financially dependent on their relatives, almost essential (Mosquera, 2006; Mosquera, et al., 2009).

Often, relatives of people with BPD are the ones establishing the initial contact searching for information. This first contact usually coincides with a crisis, after an attempted suicide or deep self-harm, in which the patient asks for help because things have gotten out of hand, or after receiving the diagnosis (Mosquera, 2006; Mosquera, et al., 2009). It is also common to receive calls asking for information when the patient is admitted because they want to take this time to receive guidance on how to help, on how the center works, or on treatment options. This initial contact usually occurs in a desperate and sometimes overwhelming manner.

At the beginning of therapy, demands from the family are closely connected with the most dangerous and destructive behaviors (suicide attempts, self-injury, aggression to other family members) and with other associated problems, such as drug and alcohol abuse or eating disorders. This may complicate the process of establishing goals, especially if treating professionals get carried away by the patient's chaos and the family's despair.

A recurring complaint by family members is that they are not told what is happening to the patient. Another one is that they do not receive specific guidelines on how to act in order to improve the situation. In some cases, they come in feeling so desperate that they are surprised when they receive an explanation or have someone talk to them. This is essential, given that families need information and specific guidelines to handle different situations that may arise (Mosquera et al., 2009).

In the initial contact, it is common for family members to ask about the causes of the disorder, since they fear, in the case of the parents, having failed at educating their children in a proper way. In addition, they often have a sense of having done something wrong, but not knowing what it is and this, obviously, makes them feel very guilty, which is one of the reasons why it is useful to offer them psychoeducation. One aspect that is interesting for relatives is to understand that there are several factors that can influence the development of the disorder and that education is not the only one. It should be remembered that there are multiple causes that can trigger BPD and cause symptoms to appear: genetic, biological, environmental, social, and situational. It is important that both the patient and the family understand that we are not trying to find out who is guilty, but instead, to explore those situations or attitudes that negatively affect the patient and the family, in order to modify them, so all members of the family unit can benefit.

With the support of the family, results can be much faster, effective, and above all durable, because they will remain in contact with the patient when the treatment has been concluded.

See appendix C for more information.

Chapter 15
Psychotherapies for Borderline Personality Disorder

While patients previously often faced a defeatist attitude in regards to the treatment of personality disorders, in recent years we have seen the development of a variety of approaches specifically aimed at personality disorders and, most notably, borderline personality disorder (BPD). The following briefly describes some of the best known.

TRANSFERENCE FOCUSED PSYCHOTHERAPY

Transference focused psychotherapy has a psychoanalytical orientation and was developed in the sixties by Otto Kernberg (1967), but has been refined over the years. As opposed to traditional psychoanalysis, the therapist plays a very active role in therapy. The patient-therapist relationship is the focus from which we attempt to get to the underlying structure of the patient's relational functioning. The main objective is to bring the patient's unconscious conflicts to the surface so they can actively be worked on between patient and therapist. In 1998, the book *Psychotherapy for Borderline Personality* (Clarkin, Yeomans, & Kernberg) was published, suggesting a psychodynamic approach to treating patients with borderline organization. It contains numerous vignettes of highly illustrative clinical cases to facilitate the understanding of techniques and methods.

SCHEMA THERAPY

This therapy was developed by Jeffrey Young throughout the eighties and integrates elements of cognitive-behavioral therapy, object relations theory, and Gestalt therapy. It focuses directly on the deeper aspects of emotion, personality, and schemas from which the individual functions. It describes several fundamental ways in which people with personality disorders categorize, perceive, and react to the world. It places great emphasis on the importance of the therapeutic relationship and the therapist's authenticity. Childhood traumatic experiences in which schemas and modes described in this approach are conceived are considered an important aspect in understanding the patient's reactions in the present, often establishing bridges between past and present that help the patient understand the relationship between what they learned and how they relate, interact, and respond to others. It can be very useful for offering psychoeducation that the patient can easily understand.

DIALECTIC-BEHAVIORAL THERAPY

Marsha M. Linehan developed dialectical behavior therapy (DBT) in the nineties, publishing two manuals, *Cognitive-behavioral treatment of borderline personality disorder* (Linehan, 1993a) and *Skills training manual for treating borderline personality disorder* (Linehan, 1993b). It was initially oriented toward suicidal behaviors. It differs from traditional cognitive-behavioral therapy in the attention placed on providing resources to the patient in order to manage emotional distress and it introduces working with social skills. The central elements of DBT are learning new competencies, including mindfulness, interpersonal effectiveness, adaptive management of anxiety and crisis, and emotional regulation. One of the main objectives of this psychotherapy is to give patients more resources so that they are able to regulate themselves emotionally. It has shown great efficiency in the management of self-harm and suicidal behavior. The therapy is very focused on the diversion of attention as a regulatory strategy and provides very interesting complementary strategies. The group application is best known, but it is also applied individually, and there are also adaptations for adolescent populations.

COGNITIVE-ANALYTIC THERAPY

This therapy emerged as a time-limited psychotherapy for application in public settings (Ryle, 2002) and integrates elements of cognitive-behavioral therapy and various psychoanalytic approaches. Its distinctive features include reformulation and its collaborative nature, which actively involves the patient in the therapeutic process. It identifies sequences of events, thoughts, emotions, and motivations that create and maintain problems. An interesting concept in this therapy is reciprocal roles, which explains how the patient's patterns interact with other individuals following a particular dynamic. Therefore, it gives much relevance to the relational aspects and not just to what happens inside the individual.

MENTALIZATION BASED THERAPY

Anthony Bateman and Peter Fonagy (2004) focus on attachment distortion due to problems in parent-child relationships in childhood, hypothesizing that inadequate empathy and attunement by parents in early childhood lead to mentalizing deficits, defined as the ability to intuitively understand the thoughts, intentions, and motivations of other people and the connections between their own thoughts and feelings and actions. Thus, treatment focuses on the development of this mentalization capacity. In this approach, the therapist-patient interaction also plays an important role.

PSYCHOEDUCATIONAL PROGRAMS

The goal in psychoeducational approaches aimed specifically at BPD is for patients to acquire greater understanding of their presenting problems and learn new skills and strategies. These programs can be targeted individually (Mosquera, 2004b) or with relatives (Mosquera et al., 2009). In these programs, patients learn to develop self-observation and self-care; to identify their defense mechanisms, problems with boundaries, and identity distortion; and to acquire skills in emotional management and coping techniques.

The overall philosophy of these programs is not to teach patients, but to help them know themselves, identify and assess their own resources and, from here, develop new and more effective skills.

EMDR THERAPY

Given the high prevalence of traumatic events in patients with BPD, therapies specifically oriented toward trauma offer interesting possibilities in these clinical pictures. One promising approach is treatment with EMDR therapy (EMDR stands for Eye Movement Desensitization and Reprocessing), an approach with wide empirical support in the treatment of trauma (Shapiro, 2001), which is starting to be applied for individuals with borderline personality disorder with highly promising results (Mosquera, 2010; Mosquera & González, 2011). In this approach, traumatic memories, including not only situations of abuse or maltreatment, but also daily experiences related to insecure attachment or adverse events of various kinds, are considered the foundation of borderline pathology. Based on the adaptive information processing model, these disturbing experiences remain dysfunctionally stored in the nervous system, blocking the innate system with which our brain processes experience. EMDR therapy consists of eight phases, including initial stages of history taking and stabilization, in order to later access and reprocess the disturbing memories.

OTHER

Several trauma-oriented therapies may be equally applicable to borderline patients, whose condition is understood in many of the approaches described above, as based on early adverse experiences and difficulties. In this sense, the Theory of Structural Dissociation of the Personality understands BPD within the posttraumatic spectrum (Mosquera, Gonzalez, & Van der Hart, 2011) and suggests specific interventions for these cases.

Related to this orientation, Sensorimotor Psychotherapy (Ogden, Minton and Pain, 2006) focuses on the somatic impact of adverse experiences, an element often neglected in other approaches that focus on the verbal, cognitive, and emotional components, integrating recent knowledge in neurobiology and elements of other types of psychotherapy.

Trauma oriented psychotherapies have common elements and are easily linkable in working with borderline patients, who require global and integrative treatment models that respond to the various areas on which the patient needs to work.

Chapter 16
Maintaining Improvement

> "... The famous centipede, to whom the cockroach innocently asked how he managed to move so many legs at once with such elegance and harmony. The centipede reflected on the matter, and from that moment on, he was unable to take another step."
>
> Paul Watzlawick (1987)

One of the most delicate steps in the process of change is maintaining improvement. When people feel more stable, they may have a hard time adjusting to their new life. Although we cannot forget individual differences and other aspects that influence therapy, usually people have learned a lot and they have made changes that greatly improve their quality of life, and their way of adapting to unexpected or unforeseen situations, as well as the way they deal with the discomfort characteristic of this disorder. They often feel much safer, less confused, less lost, more hopeful for their near future, and especially more deserving. Their feeling of guilt, which is usually present, and their fears decrease significantly and they realize that it is through talking that people understand each other. But this moment may be one of the biggest challenges for the therapist, greater than the first phase of treatment (setting boundaries, managing self-destructive behavior, suicidal crises, working with defense mechanisms, etc.).

This stage may be the most frustrating of the entire process. It is essential not to become overly confident and to be more vigilant than ever, since it is common for the end of therapy to activate many fears, for example, of taking the next step, of remaining as they have been so far, and of living a normal life.

When a person has learned to use the resources they need in order to remain emotionally stable, when their emptiness has been partially filled up with things or people with whom they feel comfortable, when they have established the habit of work or study, and, above all, when they have not yet had time to think about how or why they have successfully recovered, this is when the therapist can form the idea of starting to distance the sessions and of moving to discharge the patient. This is where we run the risk of making one of the biggest mistakes: proposing it too soon. The patient may immediately relapse, feeling as if they are being abandoned, and their insecurity, mistrust, and emotional instability may return. All this may cause and trigger an immediate crisis.

Not being used to their new situation, as well as fears of the unknown, of not being able to remain stable, of messing up and then not knowing how to fix it, and of disappointing the therapist or their relatives, all this can generate a lot of insecurity and destabilize the person with borderline personality disorder.

Given all of the above, we must be particularly cautious and, in this sense, we must adopt an almost contemplative attitude: we must stop doing. We must allow patients to be the ones who make decisions, who propose the intersession intervals, and who realize, in a natural way and attending to their own needs, that their current lifestyle does not allow them to come see us as often as they would like.

In a way, it may be similar to when children learn to ride a bike with training wheels. While they have the wheels on, they get on the bike without fear and feel that everything is under control. Seeing that their friends take off the training wheels and keep on riding their bikes, they will also want to have them removed. While many children outgrow this first fear and realize that they can continue without training wheels, others simply end up falling and feeling like a failure, due to fear of not doing well or falling. Thus, we must go slowly, letting them go as they request, never pushing for this to happen. Some parents let them go at once and there are others who tell them *"I'll hold you"* and release them gradually until the child realizes that he really knows how to do it alone. In therapy the same thing happens, although we may think that patients have already learned a lot and can continue without our support, they must be the ones who are convinced.

The wellknow children's tale *The Three Little Pigs* is a good metaphor to illustrate this process. In the story, the three little pigs decide to build their own homes in very different ways. The first little pig built his house in one day, with a bunch of straw. The second one had to work a little more, looking for reeds and pieces of wood in the forest, and finished it in three days. And finally, the third little pig dedicated many months and effort to building a solid brick and cement house with a door, windows, and a fireplace. He warned his siblings that their homes were unsafe and would not resist if the wolf showed up, but they did not pay much attention and thought what he was doing was too much effort. One day the wolf appeared. First he went to the house of straw, the most vulnerable, and with a slight puff, the house collapsed. Then he turned to the wooden house and blew, but the house did not fall, as it was a little tougher than the previous one. Then, he took an ax and cut the reeds and wood, and in this way the second house collapsed. But when he got to the third house, he realized that this one would be more difficult to bring down. He thought that with just a little effort, it would be like the others and finally fall, but he was so wrong! All those months and hard work had paid off. The house was solid, with many components that helped it be a safe place.

In this modified version of the story *The Three Little Pigs*, we see three very different pigs with one same goal: to seek protection and a safe place to live (with themselves). The approach of each one is very different, and the result in each case very different as well. If we act like the first pig, looking for easy solutions and building a straw house, the first setback will make this house vanish. In the case of borderline personality disorder, the same thing happens: If the person resorts to alcohol, binge eating, cuts, etc., discomfort seems to be covered up (like the straw house), but in reality, it is not.

If the person acts like the second little pig, looking for somewhat better solutions but not well adapted to his needs, like making a wooden house when something more is needed, this house may not disappear at once, but it will when the second or third setback come around. In the case of BPD, this can happen if patients resort to therapy or medication when they suffer an unexpected low and then drop treatment as soon as it is starting to work, or when some behaviors are replaced by others that are less harmful. They do not really work on their basic problem, which is the disorder and its allies (the wolf and its tricks).

But in the case of the third little pig, the one who builds his home brick by brick with great effort, the chances of getting a solid and secure home are much higher. In addition, if while building this house (stability) one realizes that a row of bricks is a little crooked, but instead of continuing along this path, one repositions the bricks, the possibility that this house will disappear or collapse is much smaller. Obviously, it needs some care and attention sometimes. If a window is a little loose, we must straighten it, after so much effort it cannot be neglected. This happens to all of us human beings. We all have unexpected situations and problems, but if addressed on time, they become solutions and enable improvement to be maintained (the house remains solid despite every setback).

It is important to remember that people with this diagnosis often have relapses when least expected, after they have been stable for a while, and when it seems that everything is under control. Contrary to what it may seem, increased functionality gained as therapy progresses can make the emotional conflict related to this disorder seem intolerable. All this, mixed with low self-esteem and overly high expectations of oneself and others, can trigger unexpected reactions in patients at moments of frustration or when something unexpected happens. Sometimes, this is due to pressure from the environment and fear of not being able to maintain the acquired and unfamiliar stability. One possible explanation is that during periods of instability, bad moments are nearly normal and patients are well used to them. However, when they think everything is over and their life is finally on the right track, frustration may seem intolerable, especially if they fear that everything is starting over again and they will be unable to go through it again.

Our trust in the recovery of our patients is our best ally in order to help them.

Appendix

APPENDIX A. INTERVIEW FOR ASSESSING THE PRESENCE OF A POSSIBLE BORDERLINE PERSONALITY DISORDER

Patient: _____

Therapist: _____

Date ___ / ___ / ___

CRITERION 1. Frantic efforts to avoid real or imagined abandonment.

a) Have there been times when you have felt very sad, particularly vulnerable, or alone because you thought someone you loved or needed could leave you?
b) How often has this happened?
c) What was your reaction?
d) Did you do anything to prevent this person from leaving you? If the answer is yes, explore their reactions and what they were expecting to obtain.
e) What else did you do?
f) Do you spend much of your time thinking of ways of preventing people from abandoning you?
g) If the answer to the above question is yes: Does this happen with the people that are closest to you? Does this happen with many people?
h) Why do you think this happens?

Note: *In this section, we should explore the feeling of dependency patients can have in regards to their loved ones or inquire if they have a tendency for "getting hooked" in new relationships. In addition to providing meaningful information about the first criterion, it is a way to gradually introduce the next section.*

CRITERION 2. Pattern of unstable and intense interpersonal relationships characterized by alternating between extremes of idealization and devaluation.

a) Are your relationships with friends, family and/or partners usually intense? *If the answer is yes, ask for specific examples.*
b) Do you think you tend to maintain stormy relationships with many ups and downs?
c) Can you talk a little bit about them?
d) Do you go from loving, respecting, and admiring some people to despising and even hating them, depending on the moment or the reaction of the other person? *If the answer is yes, ask them to expand on their answer a bit more.* Can you tell me about this? Why do you think this happens to you? Does it happen with people who are close to you? What about with people you have just met?

CRITERION 3. Identity disturbance: markedly and persistently unstable self-image or sense of self.

a) How would you describe yourself?

b) Do you usually describe yourself in the same way or do you change depending on the moment and even on the people with whom you are?

c) How often do you change your way of thinking about yourself?

d) Have you ever felt as if you were another person?

e) Have you ever felt as if you do not know who you are or how you are?

f) Do you have clear preferences? And what about your tastes? *Ask for examples.*

g) Do you find yourself acting differently depending on the context? *If yes, inquire about the frequency and have patients expand on the answer and give concrete examples to better understand what they are feeling and the role these changes may have.*

CRITERION 4. Impulsivity in at least two areas that are potentially self-damaging (i.e.: spending, sex, substance abuse, reckless driving, binge eating...)

Note: *Do not include suicidal or self-mutilating behaviors covered in Criterion 5.*

a) Do you consider yourself an impulsive person? *If the answer is yes, ask*: What does "impulsive" mean for you? Can you give me a concrete example?

b) At what times and in which situations may you react impulsively? *Ask for examples.*

c) Have you ever spent money on things you did not need or could not afford?

d) Have you had the need of buying or selling things and/or replacing them with others that you did not really need?

e) Have you had one-night stands or brief sexual encounters? *If yes, explore in depth how the patient has felt afterward:* Do you feel comfortable with these encounters? *In some cases, relationships are sought in order to feel falsely loved, to feel accompanied, etc., and in other cases there is discomfort associated with this behavior and the patient feels bad / guilty / dirty...*

Note: *If the person maintains sporadic encounters and enjoys it without feeling bad, if it is a clear choice, we would not consider this as an impulsive-destructive behavior, but as the preference of the patient. It is important not to let ourselves be guided by our choices and ideologies or we may unconsciously bias the response.*

f) Have you gotten drunk frequently or in situations where you knew it was not good timing? *Ask for examples.*

g) Have you ever gotten "high" or taken drugs? How often? How much? *Explore the reasons*: Do you like it? Does it help you disconnect or escape? *If the patient says the reason is to escape*: From what are you trying to escape? From what are you trying to disconnect?

h) Have you ever stolen or taken something that did not belong to you?

i) Have you ever had an accident that could have been avoided?

j) Have you ever gotten a ticket for speeding or driving recklessly, for not respecting traffic rules?

k) Have you ever taken the car and driven recklessly after an argument, or due to boredom or anger, for example?

l) Have you ever driven under the influence of any substance (alcohol, drugs, medication that interferes with responsiveness, etc.)?

m) Have you ever eaten compulsively (large amounts of food in a short period of time with the feeling of losing control, of not being able to stop)?

n) Have you ever broken things you liked and did not intend to break during or after an argument with someone close or after feeling anger or disappointment?

o) Do you often do things impulsively that can cause you problems? *If the answer is yes, it is important to ask for examples.*

CRITERION 5. Recurrent suicidal behavior, gestures, or threats, or self-mutilating behavior.

a) Have you ever thought about hurting yourself? If the answer is yes, How often?

b) Have you told someone you wanted to hurt yourself, you would like to die, or you wanted to commit suicide? Tell me about it.

c) How often have you done that? In which situations?

d) Have you done this with the same person or with different people?

e) Have you ever attempted suicide? How many attempts? What did you do?

f) Can you talk about why you have thought about suicide and death? *If they have taken action and attempted suicide*: Can you explain why you have tried killing yourself? *It is important to try to find out if the patient wanted to die or wanted to stop suffering.*

g) Have you ever self-harmed? *If yes, ask for the reasons*: Why? For what purpose? What were you feeling? What were you trying to obtain or avoid? *The idea is to explore if the patient felt relief, wanted to escape, wanted to have control of the situation, or if it was self-punishment, etc.*

h) How have you hurt yourself?

i) How often?

j) Do you remember the first time that this idea came to mind? Can you talk about it?

CRITERION 6. Affective instability due to a marked reactivity of mood (e.g.: intense episodic dysphoria, irritability or anxiety, usually lasting a few hours and only rarely more than a few days).

a) Have you ever been told that you are irritable?
b) Have you ever been told that you have mood swings, that you are very variable or unpredictable? *If the answer is yes, ask the patient to talk about it, ask about frequency and intensity (mild, moderate, severe).*
c) Do you easily go from feeling joy to feeling sadness (or vice versa)?
d) How often does this happen? In the same day, once a week, several times a week, every day, once a month, etc.?
e) How long can these moods last?
f) Do you go from feeling very unmotivated to feeling very happy and encouraged by something that may seem irrelevant to others? *If the answer is yes, ask for examples.*

CRITERION 7. Chronic feelings of emptiness.

a) Have you ever felt empty? How many times? *Explore frequency and intensity.*
b) How would you describe the feeling of emptiness?
c) Are you easily bored?
d) Do you feel that whatever you do is not enough to fill the void? *If the answer is yes*: How do you try to fill the void?

CRITERION 8. Inappropriate, intense anger or difficulty controlling anger (e.g.: frequent displays of temper, constant anger, recurrent physical fights).

a) Do you easily get angry? *If the answer is yes, explore if the anger seems appropriate and ask for some examples.*
b) How often do you show a bad temper?
c) What things or situations make you angry to the point of feeling you can lose control? *Explore whether the patient has difficulty handling anger and to which extent.*
d) Do you ever feel angry, annoyed, irritated without knowing why you feel this way?
e) Can you tell me how you are when you're angry? *Explore reactions, feelings, thoughts, etc.*
f) How long does your anger usually last?
g) Do you feel angry much of the time?
h) Have you ever broken or thrown things around?

i) Have you ever hit anybody?

j) Do you regularly engage in physical fights, even provoke them?

k) *If the answer to any of these questions is yes:* Tell me about it.

l) Do you often react by yelling, hitting, threatening or breaking things when you're angry?

m) Have you ever given other people the silent treatment instead of taking action? *If the answer is yes*: How long can you keep it up? What do you pursue with this treatment?

CRITERION 9. Transient, stress-related paranoid ideation or severe dissociative symptoms.

a) When some people are emotionally activated, they can have experiences that are very difficult to explain to others. Have you ever had this feeling? *Explore these strange experiences.*

b) When you have been under stress, have you ever felt as if your body or part of your body had changed in some way or was not real? Did it ever seem that things around you were in some way strange or changed shape or size? *If yes, ask to describe it and try to figure out when these "strange things" take place.*

c) Have you ever felt as if you were watching yourself from outside your body? *If the answer is yes, describe.*

d) Do you ever have memory lapses, feelings of not remembering what happened or of forgetting what happened?

e) When you are under stress, do you become paranoid or suspicious of people you generally trust?

f) Have you come to believe that close friends and relatives are spying on you or want to hurt you? *If the answer to any of the above is yes*: Does this ever happen without you feeling stressed?

Note: It is important to rule out that any of these experiences have emerged under the influence of any substance.

APPENDIX B. THERAPEUTIC RECOMMENDATIONS FOR THE MANAGMENT OF SELF-HARMING BEHAVIORS

1. Becoming familiar with the pattern of behavior associated with self-injury. It may be helpful to ask when it happens, how it happens, where it happens, why it happens, how it happens and what for.
2. Figuring out the pattern of self-harm (organized, disorganized, premeditated, impulsive).
3. If patients use objects to self-injure, finding out what is being used, how these objects are obtained, if they are cleaned and/or disinfected, where they are usually being kept, if they have any meaning or not, and the reasons for choosing them initially and currently.
4. Exploring the context in depth (private, public,...).
5. Finding out if patients usually self-harm alone or if they have ever done it in the presence and/or company of other people.
6. Exploring the extent of the injury and the places on the body that patients tend to injure, in order to seek medical help when the situation warrants it. Some cuts need stitches and will not easily heal without intervention. If patients do not go to the doctor, other problems may arise, as for example infections, which in extreme cases can have a very negative outcome, such as amputation of a foot or hand.
7. Helping patients identify the different emotional states that precede and follow each episode. Exploring how they feel before, during, and after self-injury.
8. Differentiating between self-harm and suicide attempts. They are very different issues, with different motivations, and each one has to be specifically addressed.
9. Finding out possible triggers for self harm with the intention of facilitating and proposing better short and long-term adaptive alternatives.
10. Finding out how patients live with their injuries: Do they hide them? Are they ashamed? Do they show them? Do they brag about them? This will provide significant information about the motivation and the reason for the behavior.
11. Confronting dichotomous thinking, helping patients take intermediate positions and expand the global view of different situations.
12. Helping patients identify their emotional responses and how their way of perceiving and interpreting different situations may influence these responses.
13. Helping patients verbalize different emotional states so they can express their feelings with words and, above all, so they can identify the feelings that usually end up in self-harm.
14. Making suggestions that patients can implement in order to manage emotional distress.
15. Developing contingency action plans for critical situations that tend to "activate" patients and make them think about self-injury. This should be done regardless of their reasons for considering self-harm, because we should remember that some do it for relief, others to "come back to reality," others to feel alive, and others to "get what they deserve."

16. Avoiding excessive alarming reactions, remaining calm, and focusing on solutions regardless of the severity of the behavior and/or injury.
17. Delving into the reasons that precede each self-harm episode, without getting into questions that may seem morbid for patients. It is important to explore in depth and show interest without being intrusive or tactless.

It is very important not to judge patients' behavior and to try to understand their feelings and the reasons that led them to act in such a destructive manner. It is also important to remember that this may be their way of coping with and tolerating pain. Another issue that therapists must manage is verbal and non-verbal language. What we say is important, as is the tone and the timing, but the gestures that accompany our words are equally important, and even more, since words of support accompanied by a critical tone or a gesture of disapproval will be useless.

There is neither a magic recipe for understanding and treating people who self-harm, nor for them to stop self-injuring, but there are some essential ingredients: understanding, information, interest, tact, calm, patience and respect. Especially, respect.

APPENDIX C. PRINCIPLES THAT MAY BE USEFUL IN INDIVIDUAL AND FAMILY APPROACHES

1. **Being extremely cautious, adapting to the patients.** We must remember that each person is a unique individual, that personal situations are unique, and that we cannot generalize or assume that interventions that work in many cases must work in all cases. This would be falling into a rigid (and somewhat narcissistic) position, in which therapists attribute excessive value to their own assistance and advice.
2. **Respecting the limitations and the pace of patients and their families.** Although we may clearly see what should be done to improve the situation, we cannot forget that our perspective is not contaminated by experiences of emotional contagion, despair and, in many cases, previous interventions that have failed. Family members need time to be able to trust again and sometimes it will be hard for them to collaborate as they would like to. They have been hurt too many times and learned to protect themselves by expecting the worst.
3. **Normalizing without invalidating.** Sometimes, with the best of intentions, patients are invalidated: *"Don't cry, it's no big deal,"* *"Do you really think you're feeling so bad for what happened with your friend?, I don't understand it,"* *"You can't let things affect you so much."* (Optional comment: *"How do you think you can get these situations to affect you less?"*)
4. **Identifying options.** It is important to help patients and their families to seek alternatives, to give them clues that allow them to reach a global view of the situation, and to offer guidelines to give them some sense of control. When offering help we must pay attention to our body language, since certain gestures may invalidate patients and confuse them (saying one thing but non-verbally transmitting another one). This is why it is useful to video record sessions, because sometimes this is done unconsciously and recordings allow reviewing details that would otherwise go unnoticed (gestures, inconsistencies, interruptions, etc.).
5. **Avoiding comparisons.** This is a way of normalizing by invalidating. Comparisons, both those related to ourselves (*"the same thing happened to me"*), and those related to others (*"your brother passed all his tests and you do not even get up to go to class"*) should be avoided.
6. **Not conveying doubts.** It is natural to have doubts, but it is very important not to transmit them. This does not mean we should not clarify issues that are unclear (see item 13). This item refers to concerns such as, *"I don't know where to go from here,"* *"Now, what do I say?"* which make sense in the beginning of therapy, but must only be shared with the treatment team, and never with the patient. On one occasion, a patient who had the same therapist for years felt like a failure and totally abandoned when the therapist told her, *"I don't know what else to do with you, I think it's better for you to get an appointment at this other center where you can get help."* (Optional comment: *"I think you've come a long way during the time that we have worked together and you can still do more, so I'm interested in knowing the point of view of another professional to see if we can get any suggestions. Would it be okay with you to ask for a second opinion from a colleague?"*)

In this way we are conveying interest, we are valuing their work and the time they have dedicated to therapy, rather than transmitting a sense of desperation and the impression that they can no longer advance in therapy. This patient came in thinking she was a lost cause, saying, *"If she does not know what to do, given that she is the one person who knows me best, then no one can help me."*

In this case, the situation was reoriented as follows: *"I think this is a misunderstanding, because she has told me you are a very brave and very capable person. She is eager to continue working with you; she believes you can give much more than you give, but she suggested we do collaborative work because we are implementing a specific program in this center with which she was not familiar. I am under the impression that her idea was to keep working as a team, supervising everything I do, since she already made it clear that her main interest is that you continue improving."* The patient felt safer and eager to move forward. And it was the truth, because her therapist with the best of intentions wanted to convey that she was the one who did not know what to do, but not that she did not know what to do with her. This nuance is an example of how important it is to be cautious and pay attention to detail.

7. **Listening, allowing patients to explain their grievances and doubts**. Sometimes, due to time constraints, we require that patients be specific with their exact complaint (something very difficult for a person with a personality disorder, especially borderline personality disorder, in which vulnerability and lack of identity can make them change overnight). If we do not have time, we can say the following: *"Time seems to be going by very quickly and I get the impression that it is not enough, is it okay if I ask you to expand this information in writing? I am interested in knowing your concerns to help you set goals that allow us to advance in therapy."*

8. **Assesment**. At our treatment center, INTRA-TP, we present patients with a biographical questionnaire that inquires about diverse information regarding different life areas. This questionnaire, which can be very laborious, often provides a sense of *"they care about what I think," "they are doing a full assessment to help me," "I'd never delved so deeply into my feelings and concerns."* It is a first step for structuring therapy and clarifying objectives.

9. **Giving feedback, not just listening**. Therapists must take an active, participatory stance. If venting is allowed and afterwards we do not give any feedback to patients, this can make them feel very bad. Without feedback, they are likely to unleash their imagination and reach to conclusions such as, *"I've surely explained myself horribly," "She doesn't know what to do with me, she must think I'm a pain in the neck," "She probably thinks I'm crazy and that's why she hasn't said anything," "How shameful, I can't come back to our next session, I told her things that I wasn't going to say," "Maybe I did it wrong, I should have asked more questions."* They may also reach the following conclusions: *"What a shitty therapist," "He doesn't know what he's doing," "What a disappointment, there I was telling my whole life story for someone to help me and I get nothing in return."* The type of interpretation patients make of this situation can be highly variable and is influenced by their emotional states, their usual defense mechanisms, transference issues, or their personal situation.

10. **Keeping calm and not taking the attitude of the patients personally**. These two aspects often are closely related. In some cases, we find extremely accommodating patients who are so depressed and confused that they are unable to defend themselves. These are patients with whom it may be easier to empathize. In this case, staying calm will be relatively simple and will come naturally to us. Then there are cases of people with this diagnosis who come in on the defensive, usually when they already have seen many professionals and are still the same. In other situations, patients who usually collaborate during sessions arrive with a defensive attitude, even an offensive one. This can confuse the therapist and generate a variety of feelings and negative countertransference reactions.

    In these situations, it is important to remain calm and not take the patient's attitudes or responses personally, to remember that this is valuable information and also part of the problem that brings the patient to treatment. This will be more useful than becoming upset and saying, *"If you continue with this attitude, I will end the interview."* An alternative comment that helps patients feel involved as team members and does not place any blame on them would be: *"I have the impression that you are on the defensive, is something wrong or is it just my sensation?"* If the patient is particularly uncomfortable and does not want to talk, we may ask, *"Would you rather we see each other another day and come back to this issue?"* One thing is to set boundaries and another one is to go in full-force and use our position of power with the patient. Countertransference reactions can be very useful if they are well managed, as they provide a lot of information and give us clues about the problems patients have in daily life that must be worked out. In addition, the feeling that is generated in us (countertransference) can help us understand how those people who are in contact with our patients may feel and offer them an explanation in order to increase awareness of how their reactions generate reactions (both positive and negative) in others.

11. **Preventing escalation**. This item is linked to the previous one: therapists may have difficulty differentiating between *"problems of the patient"* and *"(the patient) has a problem with me and is doing this to spite me."* Responses can be very variable but, in any case, will damage the patient and the therapeutic process.

12. **Fleeing from emotional contagion**. People with this condition may convince us that the best thing they can do is die. If we are sensitive people, we may feel overwhelmed, believe that we have no answers, become infected by the emotional state of patients, and then think there is no way to help them out of that state. Along with this, we risk trasmitting this to patients. This cancels therapeutic maneuverability and causes guidelines or feedback to be counterproductive.

    This is one of the issues with which therapists in training tend to have most difficulties. Emotional contagion clouds an objective point of view. Over-identifying with what the patient is saying does not allow adopting a therapeutic stance and can generate a sense of being blocked. Suddenly it seems that everything you know you have forgotten or is useless. In addition, out of fear or insecurity, emotional contagion can make us take drastic and harmful measures (unnecessary hospitalizations, for example), or invalidate patients.

Invalidation, even if done with the best of intentions, can have the opposite effect. Comments such as, *"This attitude does not help, you have to do your part,"* will convey to patients that we believe that are not doing well because that's what they want, they are not doing enough, or are not making enough effort. We must remember that in reality, if someone wants to die, they usually have great difficulty getting out of bed and even more coming to therapy.

13. **Not relying on what is obvious**. Remembering that many are protecting themselves and have a hard time delving into issues that are emotionally intolerable. Paying special attention to non-verbal language can tell us something very different from what the patient is saying. Addressing it directly: *"I worry about the sadness reflected in your eyes, it doesn't fit with what you're telling me. Is it just my own feeling or is something bothering you and you're not telling me?"*

14. **Not anticipating**. This issue is linked to the one about listening to the patient, waiting to gather all the information. Anticipation may have the effect of self-fulfilling prophecy or lead to non-neutral statements by the therapist that patients assume or accept due to their need to fit in and their common fear of displeasing, being judged, or abandoned.
    i. Therapist: *Today you're not feeling well, right?*
    ii. Patient: *Not too well* (when the patient is excited because he has been able to change something that was very important for him).

    This can make patients leave the session feeling worse and stop valuing the changes they have achieved. In some cases, in addition to not maintaining this change, they may resort to destructive behaviors they were not using anymore. This again gives us an idea of the extreme sensitivity and the need for being very tactful with people with this diagnosis.

15. **Clarifying aspects we do not understand**. If we ask patients whenever there is something we do not understand, we will be setting an example of what they can do when they do not understand something. This is very important.

16. **Knowing the usual difficulties faced by people with this diagnosis**. Everything mentioned so far and what follows will be of little use if we are not familiar with the problems patients are presenting, if we do not have answers to their questions, and if we cannot provide explanations that help them better understand what is happening to them so they can deal with it by searching for more effective solutions.

17. **Believing in the patient's capacity for improvement**. If we truly believe that our patients can improve, we will transmit this. We will be offering safety and hope. If we assume that change is possible, patients will perceive it. If our thoughts go along the lines of *"what a mess, I wonder what to do with this guy,"* thinking there is no hope, patients will also perceive it and act accordingly: unmotivated and hopeless. We cannot forget we are dealing with people who usually are hypersensitive and very intuitive.

18. **Motivating patients, instilling optimism and confidence**. This is also linked to the previous point. It is important to explain that optimism has to be realistic. Being too optimistic can make the patient feel pressured, misunderstood and even, in many cases, invalidated: *"He doesn't understand anything I said," "He doesn't understand the intensity with which I feel or the degee to which I can lose control."*

19. **Not losing perspective, treatment may be long-term.** In order to keep things in perspective, it is essential to review the goals on a regular basis and to remember the steps the patient has taken, regardless of how small they may seem to us. Therapists, as well as patients and their families, sometimes may start ignoring or failing to appreciate the changes and the effort involved.
20. **Revising priorities depending on the patients' situation.** This point is linked to the previous one, but it is important to bear this in mind in all cases, not just in those which can make us doubt the patient´s progress. Reviewing goals allows reviewing priorities and assessing what has been achieved, along with establishing new objectives as previous goals are achieved. This is especially important with families.
21. **Becoming their "memory" whenever patients or their relatives have doubts.** As mentioned in the previous point, remembering the steps taken by the patient, however small they may be, establishes the foundation for global change. This is due to their positive cumulative effect. It is beneficial to remember previous times when the patient and family have effectively handled situations.
22. **Remembering that emotions are transient.** When people with this diagnosis are not feeling well, they tend to think that *"nothing works,"* that *"all the work I have done has been useless because I'm feeling bad again."* And if there is emotional contagion, therapists may think the same. Transmitting and remembering that an emotional state has limited duration and intensity is very useful in therapy. This decreases the dichotomous view of certain and specific situations.
23. **Following a work order.** These patients need to organize their chaos and this cannot be done within chaos. Without a working structure, it is very easy to get lost and stop doing therapy; sessions can become nice chats without therapeutic results. This is not positive and will confuse patients, who will continue to come in because they perceive support, but will not solve any of the issues that interfere with their quality of life and their ability to do things and achieve goals.
24. **Following a structure in the therapeutic process.** Just as there is a need for order in the structure of the sessions, as discussed above, there is a need to organize the therapeutic process itself. We must avoid surprising patients by changing the way we work without first consulting them or explaining the reasons for this change. Sometimes, the situation requires a change, but it always must be explained to patients.
25. **Multidisciplinary approach.** If possible, we should coordinate our work with psychiatrists, social workers, and family therapists, that is, with every health professional working with our patients, so that consistent information is shared among all those who are treating them. If this is not possible, we should encourage them to clarify any questions that may come up both in therapy and in other treatments with other professionals. We should never assume that what the patient has interpreted is exactly what has happened and we should definitely not feed grudges. It is important to help them express their doubts, their anger, their annoyance, or anything that comes up for them in an effective way. This will also allow them to generalize it to their daily lives and prevent them from feeling confused because every professional tells them something different. Example: *"I don't know why she made that comment, but I believe it's very important that you ask her during your next appointment. If you don't talk about things that bother you or that you don't understand, she won't be able to help you because she will lack information."* *"Have you told her all of what you are telling me? It's important that you do..."*

26. **Adapting the techniques to patients and not trying to fit patients into the techniques**. As stated in point 1, what works for one person does not necessarily have to work for another, much less for everyone. This may invalidate patients and make them feel misunderstood, not respected, or make them confirm some of their most common thoughts: *"I can't do anything right; I'm a lost cause." "If this works with other people and not with me, it means my case is worse, more serious, and has no solution."*
27. **Gradually offering information**. Though psychoeducation is important and necessary, too much information at once can further overwhelm and confuse patients. It can also make them feel that *"I have so much work ahead of me that is not worth the effort because I will not be able to do it"* or make them perceive possible improvements as unattainable.
28. **Drawing on examples that allow patients and their relatives to assimilate the theory**. It is important to make sure they have understood what we wanted to convey. Assuming that our explanation will be easily understood by everyone is a mistake because each person is unique, as is their situation in each session and the specific needs they may have in each one of them. Hence the need for the therapist to possess the capacity for flexible adaptation.

In summary, adapting to each case and each situation and providing patients and their relatives with strategies that will allow them to better handle both daily and critical situations is essential. In order to do this effectively, we must actively involve patients: asking for their opinion; helping them feel they are part of the team, not just someone who has to be cured; and especially giving them control, helping them focus on what depends on them rather than on what depends on others.

This list of useful aspects in therapy could keep on growing, because every day we discover details that are important. As a final note, any orientation, any training or theoretical explanation, no matter how complete, needs to be complemented with experience, and this is something that comes with practice, something we learn directly from the only experts on themselves: the patients.

Acknowledgments

To every single person who collaborated in this book's edition and the previous one.

To each one of my patients: thank you for everything you taught me.

To all the professionals with whom I have been able to exchange ideas and discuss cases.

To Miriam, thank you so much for everything, for translating, for reviewing and for your support in many of the things I do. I really appreciate you at a professional and personal level. You are a wonderful human being.

To Barbs and Lisa. Thank you for being there, even in the distance. I love you guys!

To Eugenia, for everything, but especially for being a great friend and supporting me in all of my projects.

To Natalia, for your friendship. Thank you for helping me understand important things and for knowing how to always be there. You are an amazing person, I am lucky to have you in my life.

To Andrew for writing the forward. Thank you for being a great colleague, friend, and co-presenter. It is great teaching, writing, and thinking with you Andrew. Thank your for making things easy and for reviewing a lot of the work I do. You rock!

To Ana, Chus, Alberto, Paula, Raquel, Nacho, Andrea, Isaac, Sonia and Ramon. Thanks guys, without you I could not do many of the things I do. Thanks for your interest, flexibility, efficiency, teamwork, and sense of humor. You are a magnificent team.

To Paula, for your creativity, organization and support. I'm super-proud of you.

To my parents, for their support, respect, love, and understanding. For the teachings they have given me.

To Fina, for being like a second mother and taking such good care of me and my family.

To my brother, for his relevance in my life. Thanks for being the big brother that many would love to have.

To Pachi, for your love, respect, companionship and for making me laugh and enjoy life. I love you.

References

American Psychiatric Association. (2002). *Guía Clínica para el tratamiento del trastorno límite de la personalidad.* Barcelona: Psiquiatría Editores, S. L.

American Psychiatric Association. (2013). *Diagnostic and Statistical Manual of Mental Disorders: DSM-5 (Fifth ed.).* Washington, DC: Author.

Akiskal, H.S. (1981). Subaffective disorders: dysthymic, cyclothymic, and bipolar II disorders in the "borderline" realm. *Psychiatric Clinics of North America,* 4:25-46.

Bateman, A. & Fonagy, P. (2004). *Psychotherapy for Borderline Personality Disorder. Mentalization-based treatment.* Oxford University Press.

Beck, A.T., Freeman, A., & Davis, D.D. (1990). *Cognitive therapy of personality disorders.* New York: Guilford.

Bernstein, E.M. & Putnam, F.W. (1986). Development, reliability, and validity of a dissociation scale. *Journal of Nervous and Mental Disease,* 174:727-34.

Bowlby, J. (1969). *Attachment and loss*: Vol. 1. Attachment. New York: Basic Books

Bowlby, J. (1973). *Attachment and loss. Vol. 2: Separation.* New York: Basic Books.

Bowlby, J. (1980). *Attachment and loss. Vol. 3: Loss, sadness and depression.* New York: Basic Books

Braun, B.G. (1990). Dissociative disorders as sequelae to incest. In R.P. Kluft (Ed.). *Incest-related syndromes of adult psychopathology* (pp. 227-46). Washington, DC: American Psychiatric Press.

Cervera, G., Haro, G., & Martínez-Raga, J. (Eds.) (2005). *Trastorno límite de la personalidad: paradigma de la comorbilidad psiquiátrica.* Madrid: Editorial Panamericana.

Chu, J.A. (1991). The repetition compulsion revisited: Reliving dissociated trauma. *Psychotherapy,* 28: 327-32.

Clarkin, F.J., Yeomans, E.F., & Kernberg, F.O. (1998). *Psychotherapy for borderline personality.* 1st edition. Wiley.

Coons, P.M. & Milstein, V. (1986). Psychosexual disturbances in multiple personality: Characteristics, etiology and treatment. *Journal of Clinical Psychiatry,* 47: 106-10.

Dammann, G. (2003). Borderline Personality Disorder and Theory of Mind: An Evolutionary Perspective. In Brüne, Ribbert, & Schiefenhövel (Eds.) *The Social Brain: Evolution and Pathology.* John Wiley & Sons, Ltd.

Dell, P.F. & O'Neil, J. (2009). *Dissociation and the dissociative disorders: DSM-5 and beyond.* New York: Routledge.

Deutsch, H. (1986). Some Forms of Emotional Disturbance and their relationship to Schizophrenia. In M. Stone (Ed.) *Essential papers on Borderline Disorders. One Hundred Years at the Border* (pp. 74-91). New York University Press.

Erikson, E.H. (1980). *Identity and the life cycle.* WW Norton.

Fonagy, P. (2000). Attachment and borderline personality disorder. *Journal of the American Psychoanalytic Association*, 48: 1129-46; discussion 1175-87.

Gabbard, G.O. & Wilkinson, S.M. (2000). *Management of countertransference with borderline patients.* Jason Aronson JNC.

Grant, B. F., Chou S. P., Goldstein, R. B., Huang, B., Stinson, F. S., Saha, T. D., Ruan, W. J. (2008) Prevalence, correlates, disability, and comorbidity of DSM-IV borderline personality disorder: results from the Wave 2 National Epidemiologic Survey on Alcohol and Related Conditions. *The Journal of Clinical Psychiatry*. 69(4):533–545.

Gunderson, J. G. (2009). *American Journal of Psychiatry.* May;166(5):530-9. doi: 10.1176/appi.ajp.2009.08121825.

Gunderson, J.G. (2002). *Trastorno límite de la personalidad. Guía clínica.* Ars Médica.

Janet, P. (1904). L'amnésie et la dissociation des souvenirs par l'émotion. *Journal de Psychologie*, 1: 417-53.

Janet, P. (1919). *Les médications psychologiques.* Paris: Félix Alcan. English edition: *Psychological healing.* New York: Macmillan, 1925.

Kernberg, O. (1967). Borderline personality organization. *Journal of American Psychoanalysis Association*, 15: 641-685.

Kernberg, O.F., Yeomans, F.E., Clarkin, J.F., & Levy, K.N. (2008). Transference focused psychotherapy: overview and update. *International Journal of Psychoanalysis*, 89(3): 601-20.

Knight, R. (1986). Borderline States. In M.Stone (Ed.). *Essential papers on Borderline Disorders. One Hundred Years at the Border* (pp. 159-173). New York University Press.

Korzekwa, M. I., Dell, P. F., Links, P. S., Thabane, L., Webb, S. P. (2008). *Comprehensive Psychiatry.* 49(4):380-6.

Kroll, J. (1988). *The challenge of the Borderline Patient. Competency in Diagnosis and Treatment.* Norton.

Lewin, R.A. & Schulz, C.G. (1992). *Losing and Fusing: Borderline Transitional Object and Self Relations.* Jason Aronson.

Linehan M (1993a). *Cognitive-Behavioral treatment of borderline personality Disorder.* New York: The Guilford Press; 1993.

Linehan M (1993b). *Skills training manual for treating borderline personality disorder.* Guilford Press; 1993.

Millon, T. & Davis, R.D. (1998). *Trastornos de la personalidad: Más allá del DSM-IV.* Barcelona: Masson.

Monroe S.M. & Simons, A.D. (1991). Diathesis-stress theories in the context of life stress research. *Psychological Bulletin*, 110: 406-25.

Mosquera D. (2004a). *Diamantes en bruto I. Un acercamiento al trastorno límite de la personalidad.* Madrid: Ediciones Pléyades.

Mosquera, D. (2004b). *Diamantes en bruto II. Programa psicoeducativo.* Madrid: Ediciones Pléyades.

Mosquera, D. (2006). *Intervención individual y familiar en el trastorno límite de la personalidad.* XXVII Congreso Nacional de Terapia Familiar. Las Palmas.

Mosquera, D. (2007). *Desmontando corazas. El trastorno social aprendido: Un mecanismo de defensa extremo.* Madrid. Ediciones Pléyades.

Mosquera, D. (2008). *La autolesión: el lenguaje del dolor.* Madrid: Ediciones Pléyades.

Mosquera, D. (2010). Trastorno límite de la personalidad: Una aproximación conceptual a los criterios del DSM-IV-TR. *Persona*, 10(2): 7-22.

Mosquera, D., Ageitos, L., Bello, C., & Pitarch, S. (2009). *Llenando el vacío: Un espacio para la familia. Programa psicoeducativo para familiares de personas afectadas por un trastorno límite de la personalidad.* Madrid: Ediciones Pléyades.

Mosquera, D. & González, A. (2009). El apego inseguro-ambivalente y sus efectos en el adulto con trastorno límite de la personalidad. *X Jornadas de Apego y Salud Mental.* Internacional Attachment Network. Madrid.

Mosquera, D. & González, A. (2011). Del apego temprano al TLP. *Mente y Cerebro*, 46: 18-27.

Mosquera, D. & González, A. (2012). Terapia EMDR en el Trastorno Límite de la Personalidad. Monográfico de abordajes en los Trastornos de la Personalidad. *Revista Acción Psicológica.* Facultad de Psicología de la UNED.

Mosquera, D., González, A., & Van der Hart, O. (2011). Trastorno límite de la personalidad, trauma en la infancia y disociación estructural de la personalidad. *Persona*, 11 (suplemento 1): 10-40.

Novella, E.J. & Plumed, J. (2005). Difusión de identidad y postmodernidad: una aproximación sociocultural al trastorno limite de la personalidad. In G. Cervera, G. Haro, & J. Martínez-Raga (Eds.). *Trastorno límite de la personalidad: paradigma de la comorbilidad psiquiátrica.* Madrid: Editorial Médica Panamericana.

Ogden, P., Minton, K., & Pain, C. (2006). *Trauma and the body: A sensorimotor approach to psychotherapy.* New York: W. W. Norton & Co.

Paris, J. (1994). *Borderline Personality Disorder: A Multidimensional Approach.* American Psychiatric Publishing, Inc..

Reich, W. (1945) *Character Analysis.* Farrar, Strauss, & Giroux. New York.

Ross, C.A. (2007). Borderline personality disorder and dissociation. *Journal of Trauma & Dissociation*, 8(1): 71-80.

Rubio, V. & Pérez, A. (Eds.) (2003). *Trastornos de la personalidad.* Madrid: Elsevier España.

Rubio, V. (2006). Los síntomas "ocultos" en el TLP. *Psiquiatria.com*, 10 (1).

Ryle, A. & Kerr, I.B. (2002). *Introducing Cognitive Analytic Therapy. Principles and Practice.* John Wiley & Sons.

Sanjuán, J., Moltó, M.D., Rivero, O. (2005). *El trastorno límite de personalidad: un enfoque darwinista.* Buenos Aires: Editorial Panamericana.

Saxe, G.N., Van der Kolk, B.A., Berkowitz, R., Chinman, G., Hall, K., Lieberg, G., & Schwartz, J. (1993). Dissociative disorders in psychiatric inpatients. *American Journal of Psychiatry*, 150(7): 1037-42.

Selva, G., Bellver, F., & Carabal, E. (2005) Epidemiología del Trastorno Límite de la Personalidad. In G. Cervera, G. Haro, & J. Martínez-Raga (Eds.). *Trastorno Límite de la Personalidad. Paradigma de la comorbilidad psiquiátrica* (pp.17-39). Madrid: Ed. Médica Panamericana.

Stone, M.H. (Ed.) (1986). *Essential Papers on Borderline Disorders: One Hundred Years at the Border (Essential Papers in Psychoanalysis).* NYU Press.

Shapiro, D. (1965). *Neurotic Styles.* Basic Books.

Shapiro, F. (1989). Eye movement desensitization: A new treatment for post-traumatic stress disorder. *Journal of Behavior Therapy and Experimental Psychiatry*, 20: 211-7.

Shapiro, F. (2001). *Eye Movement Desensitization and Reprocessing. Basic Principles, Protocols and Procedures.* Second edition. New York: Guilford Press.

Soderberg, S. (2001). Personality disorders in parasuicide. *Nordic Journal of Psychiatry,* 55(3): 163-7.

Steinberg, M. & Schnall, M. (2000). *The stranger in the mirror. Dissociation: The hidden epidemic.* Harper Collins Publishers Inc., New York.

Van der Hart, O., Nijenhuis, E.R.S., & Steele, K. (2006). *The haunted self: Structural dissociation and the treatment of chronic traumatization.* New York: Norton.

Van der Kolk, B.A. & Kadish, W. (1987). Amnesia, dissociation and the return of the repressed. In B.A. Van der Kolk (Ed.). *Psychological trauma* (pp. 173-90). Washington, DC: American Psychiatric Press.

Watzlawick, P. (1987). *Lo malo de lo bueno.* Editorial Herder, S.A.

Wessler, R., Hankin, S., & Stern J. (2001). *Suceeding with Difficult Clients. Applications of Cognitive Appraisal Therapy.* Academic Press.

Young, J.E. (1994). *Cognitive therapy for personality disorders: A schema-focused approach.* Sarasota, FL: Professional Resource Press.

Zanarini, M.C. (1993). Borderline personality disorder as an impulse spectrum disorder. In J. Paris (Ed.). *Borderline Personality Disorder: Etiology and Treatment* (pp. 67-86). Washington, D.C.: American Psychiatric Publishing, Inc..

Zanarini, M.C., Yong, L., Frankenburg, F.R., Hennen, J., Reich, D.B., Marino, M.F. et al. (2002). Severity or reported childhood sexual abuse and its relationship to severity of borderline psychopathology and psychosocial impairment among borderline inpatients. *Journal of Nervous Mental Disorders*, 190: 381-7.

Made in the USA
Charleston, SC
16 January 2016